UGLY DUCKLINGS

UGLY
DUCKLINGS

JAPAN'S WWII LIBERTY
TYPE STANDARD SHIPS

S.C. HEAL

NAVAL INSTITUTE PRESS

Annapolis, Maryland

Cover photograph: Eastern Trader leaving Madras, India. (Dave Edge)
Back cover: Drawing by Michael Pellowe, Penzance, England

First published in Canada in 2003 by
Vanwell Publishing Limited
P.O. Box 2131
St. Catharines, Ontario
Canada L2R 7S2

Published and distributed in
the United States of America in 2003 by
Naval Institute Press
291 Wood Road
Annapolis, Maryland
21402-5034

Library of Congress Catalog No. 2002114058

ISBN 1 59114 888 X

This edition is authorized for sale only in the United States of America, its territories and possessions.

Printed in Canada

CONTENTS

ACKNOWLEDGEMENTS

AMONG SHIPPING ENTHUSIASTS THE WORLD OVER, from schoolboy hobbyists to hoary old historians, the interest in ships, the shipping industries and the sea takes many forms and is truly universal in character. A great deal of historical, operational, economic, technical and anecdotal information travels between them by every sort of modern communication method and is then concentrated by a variety of authors into books and articles in the ship enthusiast press. Ships live on in their memories and recollections are passed down from generation to generation long after any visible evidence of their passing has disappeared.

I grew up in a family where ships and maritime matters have actually been a bone of contention for almost as long as I can remember. On the one hand there were those who willingly went down to the sea in ships as seamen, ship captains, naval officers and their avid supporters, several categories of which included myself. Then there were those on the other side, those who hated the sea for all that it represented in loneliness and suffering, who would not "let a dog of theirs go to sea." These were the parents, wives and sometimes the children who fretted over the dangers faced by absent ones; sometimes they had a lot to worry about, particularly in times of war.

Despite the savagery of the Pacific War, the entirely different values of the martial Japanese and the frequently terrible suffering they inflicted on others, including Allied prisoners of war, I have not overlooked the fact that the average Japanese endured great suffering and in many instances, incredible destruction. However, as I have never seen any acknowledgement of the supportive front line role of Japanese merchant seamen either in Western or Japanese publications, I am acknowledging it here in this book. There must have been many acts of great bravery and sacrifice and the numbers lost—which equalled those of all the Allied merchant navies put together—testify to this. Those 62,000 Japanese Merchant Navy dead, as well as the almost equal number on the Allied side, are enough to give us all pause to think.

Ugly Ducklings is a blending of personal experiences and recollections with material culled in the usual manner from shipping registers, written histories and exchanges with maritime history enthusiasts. These individuals are found sprinkled around the globe in sometimes inaccessible and unheard of places and are most generous with their time and information. They are usually of a similar mind to my own and without the considerable participation of a number of them this book would not have been possible.

Without placing anyone in any order of precedence, special thanks are due to Bob Tompkins and Peter Cundall in Australia; Lauritz Hansen, Takao Wada and A. Endo in Japan; David Burrell in Scotland and Roland Webb of Vancouver and Seattle, all of whom made highly significant contributions to the available pool of information which forms the core of this book.

Others who helped, with information and sometimes with photos are A.R. Watts, Ian Walker, Mike Fellows and Mike Pellowe in England; Marcus Berger in Switzerland; John H. Wilterding, Jr. in Algoma, U.S.A.; Warren Foote in Australia; Ian Farquhar and Dave Edge in New Zealand; Hisashi Noma in Japan; and Jim Scammell and A.C. Hickling of Victoria, B.C. The last named produced the first photos of the Type A standard ship, the Liberty ship equivalent, in mint condition and as built. This might well have been on the re-inauguration of postwar service to Calcutta when few, if any, on the Allied side knew the origin of the mysterious vessel they were looking at. Any others of the ships as built have been copied from old newspaper pictures or the promotional materials put out by some of the shipbuilders. I thank them all.

One final word on the subject of photographs should be noted. Assembling photos of these ships has presented many difficulties and some are not of studio quality. First, there are few photographs portraying the ships in wartime conditions and secondly there has not been a great deal of attention paid to the ships by postwar photographers. As a result a considerable number of photos have been copied, which inevitably reduces the quality. It therefore became a matter of either using whatever source could be found for rare photos or doing without them entirely. Please make allowances accordingly.

On the matter of translation of Japanese ship names into English, at first blush there will be discrepancies between one source and another. For this reason please read the explanatory notes in Chapter Seven which address this subject in a way that will answer many queries.

A Note on Sources

In creating a presentation of the Japanese wartime emergency merchant shipbuilding effort, it has been difficult to be certain that all points have been covered. Language and translation factors have made for their own difficulties. Enquiries to Japanese owners, builders and other official sources have produced little in the way of tangible results. A little information has come from some textbooks listed in the bibliography and with the exception of Chida and Davies reference to the wartime shipbuilding program has been scanty indeed, if mentioned at all. Otherwise sources have come from enthusiasts in Europe, the United States and Australia with some valuable input having come from private sources in Japan.

It may even be that in official Japan there is little in the way of pride or interest in the wartime ships, although one book was published after the war in Japan with English subtitles. Excerpts of this have shown up and have been useful. Other than the book published by NYK, *Voyage of a Century* (Nippon Yusen Kaisha, Tokyo, 1985) which lists the company's war losses, among other items of interest in their fleet, there seems little else in the English language, other than more generalized histories where shipping receives little or no mention. Since writing this book Hisashi Noma has released his history of the Mitsui-OSK Line. (See bibliography for details.) The NYK listed the thirty Type A freighters in its fleet together with a brief reference to each ship's fate, but it neither explains their concept or has even a single photograph. It seems to be something that NYK wished to gloss over, acknowledging through the captions that the Pacific War, as they termed it, happened. Beyond that there is nothing, not even an acknowledgement that undoubtedly many fine crews were lost, just as happened with the Allies.

If I have missed thanking anyone, I apologise in advance.

S.C. Heal
Vancouver, BC
2002

INTRODUCTION

THIS BOOK IS AN ACCUMULATION OF AVAILABLE INFORMATION on the Japanese Type A, Liberty ship equivalent standard merchant ships and the more general subject of the Japanese emergency standard shipbuilding program, that has come to me over the years since the end of the Second World War, when I found myself in Far Eastern waters with the Royal Navy. It is not presented with the suggestion that it is a complete history. It is my belief that most of us on both sides of the conflict who had any experience of these ships "in the flesh" have now passed the proverbial three score years and ten. For this reason an effort to set out whatever is known about the ships and their place in maritime history has become something of an urgent task.

I have focussed particularly on the Type A standard ship because of my interest in the different standard types in the same size range designed, built and operated by the British, American, Canadian and Australian governments as a part of each country's war effort. As the author of two books on the Canadian ships, I learned long ago that wartime logistics have little relation to peacetime shipping economics. The several thousand tramp style vessels broadly described in the shipping markets as Liberty Ship Equivalents, did virtually dictate the shape of the postwar charter markets until their numbers thinned out with the passage of time and the development of newer, larger and more efficient vessels.

Comparisons between various nations' products and their level of success or failure can sometimes be seen as derogatory, although this is not my intent. In making comparisons between the Allied ships and their Japanese equivalents it must be remembered that the latter were born of a desperation even more immediate and overpowering than that of the Allies.

Japan's wartime standard ships have been described as "notorious even today and the worst models of ships in (our) history," a strong condemnation in anyone's language. A British source described them as "jerry-built," a derogatory term commonly applied to poorly built housing. Because of the unclassed, emergency nature of these ships, most historical accounts ignore or skip lightly over the Japanese Liberty ship equivalents. Perhaps this is for fear of reviving memories that most Japanese mariners and shipping men would prefer to forget. Whatever has been said, it is not the purpose of this book to add further condemnation, but rather to look at the emergency shipbuilding program and fit it into the context of the Japanese Merchant Marine and twentieth century Japanese history.

Also, there has been a need to describe the national characteristics which really came into focus with the Meiji Restoration and which had a major bearing on the difficult circumstances in which Japan worked itself into an untenable position. Thus we need to recognise the expedients she had to adopt in order to survive. At the same time, credit is given for the extraordinary way in which the surviving Type A freighters helped rebuild the postwar Japanese economy.

For example, they were built without regard to "class," meaning classification within the rules of the major classification societies such Lloyd's Register, Bureau Veritas and the American Bureau of Shipping. This meant that with the return of peace, they had to be rebuilt sufficiently to allow them to conform to these international classification society standards. As long as this "out of class" status subsisted, which was tantamount to being labelled unseaworthy in legal, commercial and marine insurance terms, cargo interests could only obtain marine insurance with a hefty rate surcharge on shipments made in these ships. As the marine insurance policy was also an integral part of most trade and marine financing operations the matter of class, or the lack of it, also affected trade banking transactions. (Despite their close association, the insurance market known as Lloyd's of London and the ship classification society that publishes Lloyd's Register are separate and independent of each other.)

The actual insurance of the ships themselves would also have presented problems. Hull and Machinery insurance (H&M) and the parallel legal liability field of insurance known as Protection and Indemnity insurance (P&I), functions in the way it does because Lloyd's and the many international insurance companies with marine insurance facilities share the risks. In its simplest form insurance on say a large fleet such as Nippon Yusen Kaisha (NYK) is presented to the market in such a way that many underwriting entities take a piece of the risk, either by direct participation in "going on the slip" or by way of simple facultative reinsurance. The "slip" is the document by which risks are first offered to underwriters. They signify their acceptance by placing their initials against the amount of risk accepted. It is the preliminary to preparation of the insurance policy. But beyond these steps the further absorption of risk is accomplished by a complex system of several different types of treaty reinsurance.

At least in Europe, it was theoretically possible during the Second World War for premium originating in Britain to have found some part of it accruing to German or Italian reinsurers or vice versa, given that the pooling of risks via these reinsurance arrangements often took place in some neutral country such as Switzerland which was, and still is, at the centre of world reinsurance markets. While Japan appears to have been largely cut off from the world insurance markets during the Second World War, it did mean that once regular peacetime connections were re-established, including marine insurance and reinsurance, such considerations as the quality of shipping became a factor in foreign acceptance of Japanese commercial risks.

It is useful to have some knowledge of Japanese national characteristics and the forces that drove the country to a war which she lost because of many miscalculations. The strong work ethic of the industrious, clever and compliant Japanese people, including the then much smaller middle class, and the wealth controlled by the *Zaibatsu* contributed to a unique set of circumstances leading to totalitarianism. Drawing on the strength of its people and the financial and industrial might of the *Zaibatsu*, the all powerful, centrally and militarily managed dictatorship used the emperor as its shield and fostered the sometimes fearsome illusion of invincibility presented by the armed forces.

The East Asian continent had been the objective of Japanese expansionary ambitions which grew alongside the "reforms" that followed the Meiji Restoration. Formosa and Korea were early additions to the newly conceived concept of a Japanese empire. China, racked with corruption, was the somnolent giant of the continent that presented a soft underbelly and a tempting target for Japanese expansion.

Beyond this, Japan's assumed enemies became Britain, France and Holland because they all possessed colonial assets and major shipping, oil, trading and banking interests that challenged the ideas of Japan's militaristic administration which saw East Asia, Southeast Asia, and ultimately Australia and New Zealand as their natural sphere of influence. The European powers were seen as absentee landlords, but centrally it was the United States whose long shadow—including its possession of the Philippines and a major commercial presence in most of the Pacific—ran counter to Japanese ambitions. If the Pacific was seen as America's backyard; it was certainly regarded by Japan as her frontyard. Japan presented a combination of circumstances that could do a lot of damage and did so, but in the longer run she could never have stood up against the forces of the free world, assuming that Germany, the other main enemy of the West, would not emerge victorious.

In the squaring-off of possible enemy against possible enemy which dominated much of naval planning between the two world wars, Germany saw Britain as its biggest potential enemy afloat, while Italy and France were regarded as the primary opponents in the key Mediterranean area, even though the British retained a strong presence there on account of trade and the fact that the region straddled the primary routes connecting Britain to its Indian Empire, Australia, New Zealand and its possessions in the Far East which centred on Hong Kong and Singapore. In the Pacific, the United States Navy was ranged against the Imperial Japanese Navy. In the main national navies, the battleship with its powerful ability to accurately lob a broadside of large calibre shells weighing many tons a distance of twenty miles or more, was still the capital ship.

How wrong this concept actually turned out to be was quickly demonstrated when air power was unleashed by Germany on a scale which sank warships and merchant shipping of all types. Air cover became the dominant consideration in naval planning that led to a downgrading of the battleship and the ascendency of the aircraft carrier as the capital ship of the future. The Royal Navy gave the world a taste of this trend with its successful aerial attack on the Italian fleet at Taranto when twenty-one torpedo aircraft, actually the venerable, old-fashioned "Stringbag", the Swordfish, sank three major warships. Nowhere was this more fully demonstrated than in the Pacific, first with the attack on Pearl Harbor and then when Japanese aircraft sank the two British capital ships, *Prince of Wales* and *Repulse*, off the east coast of the Malayan peninsula. This was underscored once again when the United States won the key battle of Midway, a contest entirely fought by the aircraft from the opposing carrier fleets, during which none of the surface ships even sighted each other. Most would agree that Midway was the pivotal battle of the war in the Pacific and the point when the tide turned disastrously against Japan.

Following "the proceedings" in Tokyo Bay of 1945, when General Douglas MacArthur accepted the formal surrender of the "Empire of Japan," to use his terminology, Japanese shipping was carefully controlled by the American occupying authority through the development of a licensing system. Visibly, this required all postwar Japanese ships to display their licence number, e.g., AO29, which was usually painted on the hull beneath or close to the bridge. It seems to have caused little disruption to the Japanese peacetime process of reopening its essential shipping routes. Initially, shipping was directed to imports of food and raw materials to rebuild the economy as there was little in the way of exports. One of the first major industries to be revived was Antarctic whaling. Whale products were an important component in the Japanese diet. Generally, Japan remained short of shipping until the peacetime output of its own yards caught up with demand; this meant that through its trading companies, it had to go into the charter market, which saw some interesting foreign ships engaged in Japan's overseas trades.

In 1951 the licensing system instituted after the surrender, which had placed restrictions on Japanese shipping, was lifted and navigation became free of the last of its wartime restrictions, leaving the Japanese shipping companies to go about their legitimate commercial business. The surviving types of ships depicted in this book made their way from the wreckage of a wartime economy in near total collapse to a postwar world where everyone was taking stock of what the war had left behind.

It is through the genius of Japanese shipbuilders and naval architects, overseen by international ship classification societies, that these ultra-basic wartime ships, little better than stripped-down boxes, were thrown together in record time. They were built in desperation with one purpose only; namely, as expendable supply ships. In spite of this beginning, they were able to function in war and later in peace with a surprising degree of reliability.

In some instances the survivors were rebuilt into relatively good-looking cargo liners, fit for peace-time service on Japan's main shipping routes. For the Japanese the war left behind a merchant marine that had become almost non-existent. All they had was a small residue of good-quality prewar shipping, a variety of small coaster type ships and a few larger types such as the surviving tankers, built as part of the emergency program, and about one-third of its surviving Type A wartime emergency ships. The Type A, of a similar size and capacity to the Liberty ship, would have been described as a "Liberty Ship Equivalent" in postwar charter markets, and in describing them I have borrowed the title "The Ugly Ducklings" from President Franklin Roosevelt's first exclamation on seeing an artist's depiction of the projected new Liberty ships in 1941.

In its original form, the Type A was truly an ugly duckling, and by comparison the American Liberty ship and the similar ships built in Britain, Canada and Australia were handsome, highly functional vessels built according to international classification rules. They became the backbone of the world tramp ship fleet until the classification rules and the marine insurance markets forced them to be phased out in the late 1960s. Twenty to twenty- four years of productive life under, in many cases, severe neglect as a result of shoestring management and operation was deemed long enough. Add to this the fact that in the twenty-four years following the war, the political map of the world saw the end of the old colonial empires and the growing dominance of two opposing forces: totalitarianism as personified by the USSR with international political ambitions and the modern free world led by the United States with its own agenda of economic imperialism. Of necessity, many notions governing shipping changed, and elementary rules of ship economics had to be reinvented in such a way as to drastically reshape world shipping.

Generally speaking, with comparable classes and employment of ships, the bigger the ship the lower the unit cost per ton of construction and the lower the cost per ton in terms of operating efficiencies. This meant that the wartime classes not only suffered the wear and tear of twenty-odd years of hard operation, they also suffered from functional obsolescence often well before their normal term of service was through. New ideas such as the bulk carrier and container ship took hold and gradually came to dominate and then drive the ordinary breakbulk freighter from the market. There is little doubt that Japanese shipbuilders were among the leaders in this transition, leading the way from the state of utter ruin following the war to world leadership in shipbuilding during the life of the longer-lived Type A standard freighter depicted here.

I have not tried to develop fleet lists and ship histories for all the other Japanese standard types. It would be a huge labour, with probably little to prove its worth beyond a highly limited audience. In focussing on the Type A, I have given attention to the group of ships with which most people in the West came into contact in the early postwar period. Even though only forty or so of the original number of the one hundred and forty built survived the war, they were extremely important to the early postwar Japanese economy. Unlike their Allied equivalents they had little bearing on the world shipping markets as their number was too small, but they served well on the revived, postwar Japanese cargo liner routes or as tramp shipping.

Where and when I delve into Japanese naval and general history, my treatment is far from exhaustive and is meant only to provide historical background to those events which shaped the need for the emergency standard ship. In this regard readers might find a number of the books listed in the bibliography useful in developing their historical research beyond the areas that have concerned me.

Japan's position and strength as a powerful leader in the world's economy has been one of the great wonders of the twentieth century. Figuratively speaking, I only saw the Japanese through a gunsight until I actually witnessed at first hand something of the collapse of their impoverished and defeated nation immediately after the war. In the nature of victory and defeat, it was easy to derive smug satisfaction in the fact that the Japanese had learned the most expensive of lessons. But to the great credit of the Japanese nation, they buckled down to rebuilding their shattered economy without enormous rancour immediately it was over. The military forces were broken and discredited and took little part in the postwar rebuilding except, like everyone else, as workers in bringing it about. Except for a small, surviving naval defence force, the remainder of the proud Imperial Navy became scrap to feed the steel mills. The salvage of sunken ships became a regional industry, and wherever possible Japan claimed and recovered the remains of their vessels, as if returning war dead to their native land.

Enmity and bitterness were quickly replaced with a stoic and strongly pragmatic approach to reconstruction. The fabled Japanese work ethic infected all classes and in a variety of ways has shown the way to others, notably the so-called tigers of Asia: South Korea, Hong Kong, Taiwan, Singapore, Malaysia and Thailand. Japanese commercial interests are found worldwide and the names of the old *Zaibatsu* remain, prominent as always, and enter our homes and workplaces with uncommon regularity. At one time, particularly between the two world wars, Japanese goods were often regarded as cheap and shoddy copies of the products of other countries, cynically dumped in overseas markets as a means of earning foreign currency with which to build the nation's industries and war machine. Today, Japanese brand names for everything from cars to watches and heavy machinery, from ships to computers and electronics are known and trusted everywhere, synonymous with first-class functional design and excellent quality.

Despite this resurgence by Japan since the end of the Second World War, there has been something of a malaise in the Japanese economy in the last decade of the twenty-first century. Its banking system has been heavily criticised for the cronyism and favouritism that have reaped their own rewards in the form of bad loans and an economy and political system shaken to their roots. Whatever the problems, the Japanese are a resilient people and I do not doubt that they will overcome their recent economic setbacks just as they overcame their total defeat in the Second World War.

Delagoa Maru. In the 1920s and 30s large quantities of cheap, often low quality consumer goods were dumped by the Japanese trading companies in world markets to raise foreign currency. Here a regular NYK steamer in the North European service is seen in the River Mersey at Birkenhead. Her cargo would have included toys, trinkets, textiles and ceramic products. This ship was rated as a cargo liner of 7,000 grt, built in 1919. NYK was associated with the Mitsubishi *Zaibatsu*. (John Clarkson)

CHAPTER ONE

THE ZAIBATSU: JAPAN'S FORM OF CONGLOMERATE ENTERPRISE

UNTIL THE TIME OF COMMODORE MATTHEW PERRY'S VISIT TO JAPAN in 1865 while in command of a small US Navy squadron, Japan was a feudal state largely closed to the West except for limited connections with Holland, China and Korea; the latter two in particular were trading partners. Both Portugal (which brought Christianity to Japan on a very limited basis) and Holland had colonial possessions in the East Asian region, which probably accounted for the connections. Japan had adopted its script from China and, while both were Oriental peoples, their traditions and values varied widely and one could be readily distinguished from the other by Westerners.

Perry bore an invitation from President Millard Fillmore inviting Japan to open its ports to foreign trading ships seeking bunkers and supplies and to trade with the United States. It was an invitation that the Japanese samurai class—headed by the shoguns, the warriors who ran the country—were not happy with but it was, in effect, the first tentative opening of the door to foreigners. It was also the first step by which Japan was encouraged to enter the modern world of the nineteenth century. In many ways Japan was 200 or more years behind the West and a few people in Japan realised this and saw the need to modernize.

Naples Maru. Between the two world wars Anglo-Japanese foreign trade included Japan's imports of kaolin clay used in the production of the finest ceramics. The ship is seen here in Kawasaki Line colours, at Fowey, England awaiting a berth at the clay loading dock in the early 1920s. She is an example of a Kawasaki "stock boat," or standard type steamer. These were built soon after the First World War in large numbers. They were basic flush deck tramps with few refinements. When Japan entered the war there were hundreds of similar steamers spread among her various ownerships, but very few survived the war. (Heal Collection)

San Francisco Maru. Where East meets West. Here a sister ship lies at anchor at Fowey. The two pictures of this ancient port show a scene that has no doubt greatly altered since they were taken around 1925. In the first picture old schooners lean against the stone quays. Old stone buildings and a church can be seen, with a pastoral scene of farmland and grazing cattle in the background. (Heal Collection)

The West, meaning in those days the United States and the five leading colonial powers; Britain, Spain, France, Portugal and Holland, had been fighting their own territorial and colonial wars and opening up vast regions of the world for 400 years, since the Portuguese navigators Vasco da Gama, Bartholomew Diaz and Ferdinand Magellan had led the way. Japan was however an enigma which defied Western ideas of colonialism and trade and remained a tantalizing challenge. Since its first contact with Europeans, Japan had been seen as a stand-alone nation with fierce ideas about its independence—ideas which remain a cornerstone of its existence to this day.

This opening chapter makes some observations about the organization of capitalism in Japan and compares it with similar driving forces in England, the United States and later and very briefly, Korea. It will also serve as a background for a general description of how certain major Japanese corporations with their vast resources of capital and organization, did the bidding of Japan's military and political leaders at every stage of her wars with China, Russia and later the United States, the British Commonwealth, Holland and their allies. The mounting of Japan's wartime emergency standard shipbuilding program is dealt with more specifically later on. In effect, while it may now seem to be a relatively minor event in relation to all the major events which made up the history of the Second World War, it was a factor in the very survival of Japan, and, while there are parallels with the Allies, comparisons can be made as to how each nation handled its challenges.

The discussion focusses on the *Zaibatsu*, a word equivalent to the English term "combine," as used in business and industry. The American preference is to apply the word "conglomerate" and both may be taken to mean the same thing in practice even though combines, conglomerates or *Zaibatsu* can take many forms and cover a wide range of commercial endeavours.

All such combinations are formed to take advantage of the economics of scale and concentration of capital. This means increased purchasing power, enlarged market share, the reduction of cost and the maximization of profits, all of which add up to greater economic clout. Added factors could be a desire for market domination or out and out control of a given market in the form of monopolies. In the case of the *Zaibatsu* the whole process—even though made up of about twelve groups, at least in theory competing with each other—came as close to total monopoly and control of an entire nation's people, resources, military and government establishments as has ever occurred in the history of any capitalist state. "Control" means, in this case, a position of such power that the government or its military could not function without the *Zaibatsu*. It has been equalled or exceeded only by the state capitalism of the major communist powers, but without the efficiency exercised by the *Zaibatsu*.

When Britain emerged victorious from the Napoleonic Wars in 1815, most large scale organized business and trade was undertaken by monopolies that had been granted by Royal Assent during the previous two hundred years. They slowly lost their importance over the years until by the 1830s any semblance of monopoly had faded. This was how the East India Company and the Hudson's Bay Company came into being, accompanied by others less well known and not as successful, but all seeking advantage from the processes of colonization and developing the wealth created from colonial endeavours.

Possibly the first venture was the Virginia Company (1606-1624). It sent colonists from England to establish settlements on the James River and start up an agrarian enterprise, which led to the large scale growing of tobacco, in what became the modern American state of Virginia. A later company whose main purpose seemed to be the satisfaction of the public appetite for speculation was the South Sea Company, founded in London 1711, which gave rise to the infamous "Bubble" of 1720 that cost the private fortunes of a great many people when it collapsed. The British North Borneo Company was one of the last to be organized and also the last to be absorbed into a formal government at the end of the nineteenth century. The greatest in colonial times were the East India and the Hudson's Bay Companies, the latter being the only survivor in modern corporate form of these earlier efforts at monopoly capitalism. England was not alone in this type of endeavour. The French, Dutch and others organised their colonial trading ventures in much the same way.

By the end of the Napoleonic Wars the Industrial Revolution had started in Britain and throughout the nineteenth century it was to sweep the world. War always provided a boost to technology and during the Napoleonic Wars the large-scale manufacture of armaments had grown out of all recognition. Brass and iron cannon had been manufactured for centuries, since the invention of gunpowder. Thus, a long-established foundry industry turned its attention to other activities because of the reduced postwar demand for armaments. The steam engine had been invented and steam-power became the key to ongoing industrialization throughout much of Europe and North America. During the early nineteenth century, the opening up of coal mines and metal mining grew apace and led to many other activities. With the need to bring in raw materials and carry exports to the ports, railways became giant networks of steel supporting their own particular manufacturing industries by way of rail, locomotive and rolling stock builders. Overseas British shipping likewise grew at an extraordinary pace so that by the end of the century Britain possessed the largest merchant marine and shipbuilding industry in the world, having led all others.

The move towards creating larger corporate units for different enterprises, often called "cartels," went on steadily, and the tendency to grow larger by merger continues to this day. The growth of investment trusts took hold on a large scale in England and Scotland. An investment trust held shares in many other enterprises and one could buy a stake in, perhaps, North American railroads, or South African gold mines by buying stock in a London or Edinburgh based trust which claimed to offer a better security than direct investment. In honestly run trusts this was possibly true.

The trusts appealed to the Victorian mind, with the emphasis more on security and safety and less on the philosophy of the bottom line. Maximized accounting principles such as depreciation, liquidity, asset management and the like were barely understood by the average small investor, who thought in terms of safe dividends. Most investment trusts had the objective of safety through diversity, as being a better investment strategy to have holdings in twenty railway companies than two, for example, and that principle still applies in today's investment management of mutual funds.

However, it was through investment trusts that certain British capitalists built up huge assets and controlled shipping enterprises beginning in the late nineteenth century. Two of the most successful were Christopher Furness of what became Furness, Withy & Company and John Ellerman. Ellerman formed his combine around the turn of the century, and it eventually unified its several shipping enterprises bearing his name under the common corporate name of Ellerman Lines. A third was the Royal Mail group headed by Lord Kylsant, who had close connections with Harland & Wolff, the Belfast ship-

Ryokai Maru. Japan from time to time had been a big buyer of secondhand foreign tonnage. This tramp ship, the ex-*Oristano* of 4,643 grt, was built in Britain in 1911. Seen here she appears to be calling at Capetown to unload a deck cargo of Canadian softwood lumber, which found a major market in South Africa. (Heal Collection)

France Maru. Owned by Kokusai Kisen KK. This company made a specialty out of the carriage of silk. In this instance *France Maru* is at moorings in the River Fal, near Falmouth, England. Kokusai Kisen merged with Mitsui in 1943 and this became part of the later Mitsui-OSK group. (Heal Collection)

Paris Maru. Osaka Shosen KK acquired this Cammell Laird, Birkenhead-
built ship in 1921. Of 7,197 grt, the ship shows her British origins with the
infilled crosstrees. Typical Japanese practice was to leave an open "see-
through" framework above or below the crosstrees, a feature generally not
used by non-Japanese builders. The ship is seen here at an East African port.
(Heal Collection)

Choyo Maru. The inverted frames of the crosstrees are visible in this picture of the Toyo Kisen KK *Choyo Maru* leaving Vancouver in 1928. The ship of 5,455 grt was built in 1919 by Asano. As she is not loaded to her marks she was probably on her way to a BC outport to top up with the balance of her deck cargo. Toyo Kisen became part of the Showa Kaiun group. (Vancouver Maritime Museum [VMM])

Kosei Maru. A motor vessel of 6,668 grt built in 1933, this diesel lumber carrier was owned by Hiroumi Shoji KK, which eventually became part of the Japan Line group. With her derricks seated high on the masts which themselves are erected on high mast houses, the ship was clearly designed to load big deck cargoes without impeding the use of the derricks. (VMM)

builders. Royal Mail represented an enormous bloc of shipping capital until the group fell apart in the Depression of the early 1930s and Kylsant went to prison over a falsified prospectus.

It was probably J. Pierpont Morgan, the American financier, who showed the way towards a vastly larger type of amalgamation within entire industries. Morgan saw nothing but a waste of resources in having many small enterprises competing with each other. He much preferred the clout that could be developed by bringing together large corporations which could control an entire industry, whether national or international—such as U.S. Steel Corporation, created by Morgan out of several large American steel producers.

Another of Morgan's enterprises, although somewhat less successful, was the American domiciled International Mercantile Marine (IMM) which, through its investment in and control of the White Star Line, was actually the main beneficial owner of the *Titanic* when that "unsinkable" liner sank in 1912 following a collision with an iceberg. This, incidentally, was one of the first examples of a multinational business where ownership interests bridged two or more nationalities. In this case the Belgian-flagged Red Star Line could be added to the British and American components of the IMM.

Earlier entrepreneurs of similar stature were John D. Rockefeller and Cornelius Vanderbilt, who used the same tactics for American oil and railways. So successful were they that much of the strength of American industry was attributable to these moves, but as with everything of a similar nature, private enterprise eventually clashed with public interest, particularly in the United States. The tendency to break up monopolies and promote competition has been a feature of U.S. anti-trust policy ever since.

Kashu Maru. By contrast, the high deck load on a conventional freighter requires the securing of the derricks upright against the mast with the derrick heads secured to the crosstrees. *Kashu Maru* of 5,460 grt, built in 1919, was owned by Fukuyo Kisen KK, a small trampship company which evidently did not survive the war. (VMM)

The most famous breakup was that of Rockefeller's control of the Standard Oil Trust which was broken up into no less than thirty units around the world. Doing so gave the impetus for other budding giants like Shell, Anglo-Persian (later British Petroleum) and Texaco to spread their wings. Recent examples of anti-trust action have been American Telephone & Telegraph (AT&T) and Microsoft.

Sir John Ellerman was probably one of the most successful entrepreneurs of the late nineteenth and early twentieth century to employ legal and accounting principles which, if not a model for the Japanese *Zaibatsu*, had some remarkable similarities. The *Zaibatsu* were possibly not familiar with him except that his ships regularly called at Japanese ports and competed on many routes with the Japanese companies. Ellerman had an astute eye for an investment and, with his accountancy training, could quickly scan a balance sheet and glean from it information which he combined with his exceptional knowledge of business. He made fast, astute decisions that were invariably fair and left something on the table for the other side. Ellerman formed a series of investment trusts, the first being the Brewery & Commercial Trust in 1890. At least five others followed, along with marine insurance companies. He took an early interest in breweries and, at one point in 1918, held interests in over seventy such companies in Britain, the United States and South Africa. As a large purchaser of coal bunkers for his ships he acquired collieries in Durham and South Wales and maintained large bunkering depots at Port Said, Egypt and Karachi, then an Indian port.

Ellerman's investment trusts gave him the financial strength to create one of the biggest and most successful of such conglomerates. It was virtually impregnable against predators as he personally controlled the key equity positions through holdings of deferred shares, which gave him powers that assured

Keisho Maru. Another example of a design featuring special attention to the needs of the lumber industry. This ship was built by Uraga in 1929 and owned by Showa Syosen KK which became a part of Yamashita Kisen KK before the Second World War. (VMM)

Ypres Maru. Lloyd's Register records that this vessel was built in 1920 by Tenkuku S.S. Co. at Harima although she was registered to Dai Nippon Yengyo KK. Here she is seen loading grain at Vancouver. The funnel marking is not that of Kawasaki. Naming the ship after a First World War French battleground seems an unusual choice, but reflected popular sentiment at the time. (VMM)

control by virtue of special voting rights that would not be considered legal in most jurisdictions today. He put his shipping empire together in the period from the end of the nineteenth century to the Great War, when he acquired the Wilson Line of Hull. With that acquisition his was really one of the great shipping empires of the era in the West; but it paled into insignificance alongside the industrial and financial juggernauts which were the *Zaibatsu*. However, it was the concentration of absolute power in the hands of one man which eventually led to the group's breakup. John Ellerman's death left a huge gap in the corporate fabric, and punitive British estate and inheritance taxes weakened it further. The Ellerman name exists now only as a brand name in the services of the Andrew Weir shipping group.

Conglomerate enterprise, American style, developed some strange combinations after the Second World War. American competition laws worked against the formation of vertically organized enterprises as they were considered, from past experience, monopolistic in nature. Instead, the modern American conglomerate in the postwar period tended to develop horizontally into unrelated industries to avoid anti-trust action; in other words, while competition within an industry was not seen as being reduced, the whole emphasis was on reorganizing assets and gaining leverage on equity by judicious use of debt instruments. It led to such ultimately unsuccessful groupings as United States Lines which became a subsidiary of a conglomerate, formed around a sprinkler system manufacturer, the Walter Kidde Company, only to slide eventually into bankruptcy.

In Japan, which had never developed along Western democratic lines, development took a different turn in the early formation of capital in the nineteenth century. First, it had a large peasant population who were not only compliant but also had no say in matters of state or policy. During the shogunate era, there were four distinct classes which might be said to comprise the Japanese establishment. At the top were the warrior class, the samurai, and beneath them were the farmers who produced the rice that was issued to the samurai as salaries. Rice being the staple of the realm, it was a powerful economic factor and enabled the samurai to exert economic clout. Then followed the merchants who produced wealth through mercantile activities, which in the Japanese concept meant "without personal sweat," and then came the manufacturers, who contributed little to the samurai. In Western eyes this seemed somewhat exotic and Japan and the Orient was an area of fascination for Western cultures. Nonetheless, the samurai were true products of a feudal system which Britain and much of Western Europe had more or less abandoned by a process of evolution. This growth had gained speed following the French Revolution and the adoption of a new democratic constitution by the infant United States, which set the style for others.

Here can be seen the seeds of Japan's future aggressive war against the West. Having been a feudal autocracy with almost God-like powers vested in the Emperor, Japan's real power lay with the shoguns from 1192 to 1867. These were the hereditary military commanders, each with a given district and the power of life or death over their vassals, which included everyone below their rank. This was a concept that lived on in the descendants of the samurai in the modern Japanese military dictatorship of the twentieth century. It was also the justification for the summary executions of POWs which are known to have occurred, plus the widespread ill-treatment of prisoners in their transportation by ship and in slave labour camps.

The Tokugawa shogunate, centred at Edo (now a part of modern Tokyo) was the most powerful, but the power of the shoguns was broken in the 1860s with the aid of lower class samurai from four clans

Toyama Maru approaches a berth in Vancouver Harbour in 1929. Built in 1915 by Mitsubishi for its affiliate NYK she might have been offered as proof to the Western Allies that Japan was fully capable of building first class ships. By 1917 similar ships were being delivered to the British government. (VMM)

Vancouver Maru. Kokusai Kisen KK owned this conventional freighter, built by Kawasaki in 1919 and rated as a Kawasaki "stock boat." (VMM)

centred around the Satsuma *han*, out of more than a hundred. This led to the Meiji Restoration when the Mikado or Emperor was restored as both the functional head in addition to the divine symbol of state. The Emperor had the power to appoint ministers who wanted to see a modern state structure more in line with Japan's perceived need to leave the old world of feudalism and enter the modern world. There it could compete with the West and, through its own strength, could remain independent without falling under the spell or domination of America, Britain or other countries of the West. To do this in one giant leap forward from a feudal state to a centralist, capitalist economy, Japan used its old institutions including the Shinto religion and its military tradition based on the invincibility of the samurai, as the main props in supporting the new state. This, of course, did not prevent the Japanese from imitating and adopting as their own, some western institutions and practices such as modern banks, heavy industry and the taxation policies to support it all.

Those merchants who had supported the restoration were rewarded with government support for monopolistic enterprises in various fields. Monopoly bred wealth and wealth grew into economic power in the form of the *Zaibatsu* who became the backbone of almost all Japanese business. However, those who did not support the reformers in bringing about the restoration could not be *Zaibatsu* and, therefore, did not participate in the creation of monopolistic wealth. It was an arrangement that could not last forever, as subsequent events proved, and major new industrial giants like Sony, Toyota, Honda and Matsushita grew up outside of and beyond the immediate control of the *Zaibatsu*.

Japanese capitalism owes its modern start to a wily bureaucrat, Masayoshi Matsukata. At some point around 1871 he visited France to examine its taxation methods. In 1881 he became minister of finance at a time when Japan's finances were in poor condition, but once in power he was able to incubate the idea that out of taxation revenues the country could foster new enterprises with the aid of British, French and Dutch management. The taxation revenue came primarily from land taxes, a process learned in France. The taxation was heavy and vicious, and primarily affected the poor, the peasants and small landowners. Faced with heavy taxes which many could not pay, they tended to flock into the rapidly growing cities in order to man the factories and shipyards. It was not a popular process, but probably paid better wages as the industrial economy advanced much faster than the land-based agrarian economy.

Taxation could be likened to that policy applied by the communists in the Soviet Union during the Stalin period fifty years later, when huge populations were moved around like chessmen without any power to protest. Although one was a communist policy and the other a capitalist one, both were rooted in a common need and objective, that of large-scale industrialization in an essentially totalitarian state in an effort to catch up with the West.

The enterprises chosen for support were mostly those involving heavy industry: foundries and steel production, shipyards, armament makers, and metal mining and smelting industries. Lighter industry—such as ceramics, textiles and food manufacture—was left with the merchant class, whose reluctance to invest in heavy industry had caused the government to fill the breach as part of the new, deliberate program of trading and competing with the Western World. The merchant founders of the *Zaibatsu* combined with the samurai class and had much of their new capitalist enterprises handed to them by a government anxious to foster commerce and industry. It was the start of a trend which saw government control of industry commencing in a more or less benign way until, by the 1930s, government direction had become a part of the doctrine of modern militaristic Japan, with the government in turn being largely controlled by the militarists.

However, as the *Zaibatsu* grew in power they extended themselves into all manner of industries and businesses so that by one means or another, their control spread through the entire nation. The Mitsui clan had been successful merchants and traders since 1616 when Sokubei Mitsui had forsaken his samurai roots, effectively demoting himself and his family into the merchant class. Sokubei had seen the greater opportunity that would develop for shrewd merchants, given time. He set out to be a brewer of sake and soya sauce and from that start the giant Mitsui concern developed over the following centuries. Mitsubishi, controlled by the Iwasaki family, came into being after the Meiji Restoration as did Yasuda, respectively the second and fourth in order of size after Mitsui. Number three, Sumitomo, was the only other *Zaibatsu* which predated the restoration. The others that developed later were Asano, Furukawa, Kawasaki, Otani and Okura, and all appear to have been started by former samurai or their descendants.

In 1937, Mitsui had assets of US$470 million in the value pertaining at that time but controlled many billions. The smallest of the first four, Yasuda, only had assets of US$35 million by 1945, but controlled a huge spread of investments and corporations totalling over US$10 billion. Mitsui and Mitsubishi had a massive stake in shipbuilding and shipowning, Sumitomo was dominant in metal mining and metal trading. Yasuda had large holdings in insurance and each of the four controlled its own major bank, out of a total of seven major banks, and also controlled a wide range of other businesses. There were of course lesser *Zaibatsu*, like Kawasaki, who grew in like but smaller manner, but several of these which are really postwar corporations are now giant organizations on a world scale including such concerns as Sony, Matsushita, Honda and Toyota, all symbols of today's post-war Japan. Previously insignificant organizations like Marubeni-Iida, C. Itoh and others centred particularly in the Kansai district, the dominantly cotton-spinning area of Kobe, also developed greatly with the postwar surge of Japanese growth. However, it is a reasonable assumption that one or more of the big four *Zaibatsu* have some investment interest or influence in these postwar enterprises.

Control of business, finance and industry by the four biggest *Zaibatsu* was far more comprehensive and all-embracing than anything existing in the West. Their importance to the war machine of Japan was demonstrated by the fact that they controlled 15 percent of industry related to war preparation in the 1920s, but by 1941 this percentage had risen to 72 percent. By 1945 the twelve largest *Zaibatsu* led by the four named above, controlled 75 percent of all Japanese industry, commerce and finance.

In the case of Mitsui there were the directly controlled subsidiary/holding companies bearing the name Mitsui, each of which controlled a phalanx of subsidiaries in its own right as well as having some sort of control over many others through interlocking directorships and cross-shareholdings. They were organized like a huge solar system, with the central holding company being the sun and each of its principal divisions being a planet, each of which had smaller moons circling it. The influence of the name was enough to identify a company as being a part of the group if they worked, perhaps, as subcontractors to a Mitsui company. Identification with a group at some level was also possible through the banking connections of a given company, so that to be a client of Mitsui Bank might also indicate more than a passing connection with some other of the Mitsui family of companies.

Usuri Maru lies alongside a grain berth at Vancouver. She
was owned by Nippon Kisen KK, a company that
eventually was absorbed into what became the Showa
Kaiun group. (VMM)

The "wheels within wheels" aspect of Japanese business was something far more pervasive than the "old boys clubs" of the West. The same considerations applied with the other *Zaibatsu*, and were in fact a continuation of an economic feudalism in modern corporate guise, for the Japanese had a propensity for taking from the West whatever appealed to them and mixing it in with their own particular ideals and objectives to bring about something that remained uniquely Japanese.

In shipping, the Nippon Yusen Kaisha (NYK) was, and remains, the largest and most powerful Japanese shipping line among several of the biggest on a world scale. Unless one knew its history it could be difficult to identify with one of the *Zaibatsu* and yet it is in the Mitsubishi group. One or both of its two founding components, Kyodo Unyu Kaisha and Mitsubishi Kaisha date back to 1871 when Matsukata was bringing Japan into the modern capitalist world. The two companies amalgamated in 1885 and the unified company retained its lead, as it still does as the largest of Japan's shipping groups. NYK as No.1 and the other major shipping company, Osaka Shosen Kaisha, (OSK) as No.2, maintained close working alliances. OSK is a part of the Mitsui group. NYK and OSK are the *shasen*—which might be described as the "chosen and most favoured"—mail subsidy and passenger carrying companies which historically grew up alongside each other. As first and second among the Japanese shipping companies, they were the national flag bearers on Japan's main trade routes around the world. There was only one other *shasen*, Toyo Kisen, but it transferred its ships to NYK in the difficult trading conditions that followed the First World War.

The rest of the Japanese shipowning companies were classified as *shagaisan*, which literally meant "outsiders". These had often started as struggling concerns, sometimes dominated by an outstanding individual, such as Kamesaburo Yamashita who founded the Yamashita Kisen KK in 1904; and Teiji Ishida, formerly a member of Mitsui Bussan's shipping department, who set up Taiyo Kaiun KK in 1917 and Daido Kaiun KK in 1930. Ishida was backed by Masanosuke Tanaka, formerly of Yamashita Line who had fallen out with K. Yamashita in a dispute over investment policy.

The other important *shagaisan* included Kawasaki Kisen KK, known throughout the shipping world as the "K" Line; it was founded in 1919 to own and manage a post-war fleet of ninety-six more or less identical standard freighters known in Japan's shipping industry as "stock boats". These ships, referred to later in this book as Kawasaki-type standard ships, were built by Kawasaki Kisen's affiliated ship-building company, Kawasaki Zosen. They were a continuum of the first world war program of ship-building for the Allies. When the program was overbuilt by this aggressive shipbuilder, absorbing these stock boats into the market became a major problem. Kawasaki Kisen and Kawasaki Zosen took an interest in a new company also established in 1919, Kokusei Kisen, and contributed a number of their surplus vessels to the new concern. Both shipping companies traded until 1927 as "K" Line. In 1927 both "K" and another large Japanese concern, Suzuki Shoten, got into trading difficulties. Suzuki had managed ship operations for the Kawasaki companies and by 1926 was operating 103 ships with a total

Koshin Maru. Built·in 1924, the ship is shown arriving in ballast in the late 1920s, probably to load grain. At 6,057 grt. she is small by today's standards, but with her wall like sides she gives an impression of size. Owned by Hiroumi Kisen KK she was at the time under charter to Toyo Kisen and is wearing the charterer's funnel colours. Hiroumi eventually was absorbed into NYK in the 1950s. (VMM)

tonnage of 790,000 deadweight tons (dwt). Suzuki's rise to a position as one of the biggest *Zaibatsu* had been accomplished over a short period of time during which it had acquired control of a number of industrial companies including Harima Shipbuilding Company. When Suzuki collapsed, the main beneficiaries were Mitsui and Mitsubishi whose banks held sufficient collateral against loans advanced to the Suzuki group to pick up the pieces they wanted. Harima was eventually merged after the Second World War into Ishikawajima to become Ishikawajima-Harima Heavy Industries. As such it remains as one of the foremost shipbuilding companies and close to the Mitsui group.

When Suzuki went into bankruptcy in 1927, Kawasaki Kisen went its separate way as did Kokusei, but the latter was absorbed into OSK in 1937.

The distinction between the *shasen* and *shagaisan* was an interesting one. It was simple enough in its concept with "favoured" and "outsider" companies being identified as above, but as time went on between the wars and as the highly profitable first world war period gave way to the troubled times of the 1920s and early 1930s, expedients were tried which complicated this simple relationship. Even though NYK was allied with the Mitsubishi and OSK with the even more powerful Mitsui *Zaibatsu*, the trading arms of each combine still found it expedient to develop their own shipping companies which operated within the *shagaisan* group. The *shasen* and *shagaisan* arms of each of these two *Zaibatsu* were in technical competition with each other, although in reality they mostly operated in different sectors of the shipping market, the former on passenger, mail and cargo liner routes and the other in the tramp markets. The rationalizing mergers of 1964 ordered by the Japanese government put an end to this dual relationship as NYK and OSK each absorbed their parents' *shagaisan* shipping arms as mentioned below.

An interesting situation developed with the Japanese tanker industry. The Iino Shoji company built its business as the prime coal contractor to the Japanese Navy and as the navy developed an increasing need for oil Iino grew with this need, establishing Iino Kisen in 1922. Iino was a pioneer in the development of high-speed tankers carrying California and Texas crude to Japan. In 1944 Iino Shoji and Iino Kisen amalgamated. In the meantime Mitsui took an interest in the tanker market in the late 1930s as the navy's need for tanker tonnage grew, but NYK stayed out of that market until well after the Second World War.

There were of course a considerable number of smaller companies which grew out of the *shagaisan* division into ship operating and ship owning companies. Many of these companies appear to have been formed in the late 1930s, particularly in 1937, when Japan went on a buying spree and acquired foreign-owned tonnage. There appears to be no official explanation of this policy, although Japan had been moving onto a war footing since the China Incident of 1934 when it entered into continuous conflict with China. It was most probably a strategic move to increase her merchant shipping resources in anticipation of an enlarged war. A number of these smaller companies were set up to own, rather than operate ships, leaving the management of their vessels to one or another of the strong well-established groups. Commonly, the managing group took an interest in some of these minor companies, often to the extent of holding a minority interest in the junior company. It was another way of raising capital without diluting the structure of the central managing company.

To show the extent to which the Japanese government intervenes far more than any government in the West, one only has to consider the situation at the beginning of the container age, which gathered real momentum in 1964. Twelve large Japanese lines were forcibly combined by government legislation into six major groupings so that they would be better able to handle the huge new investments that came with containerization. Thus we now have:

NYK, which merged with Mitsubishi Kaiun, a sister company in the Mitsubishi group, and the combinations of:
Mitsui-OSK,
Japan Line, (Nitto Shosen and Daido Kaiun),
Showa Kaiun (Nippon Yusosen and Nissan Kisen),
Yamashita-Shinnihon,
and Kawasaki-Iino.

The last two were soon shortened to Yamashita and Kawasaki for operational purposes.

During the Second World War and the events leading up to it, the *Zaibatsu* played a dominant role as the principal suppliers of all manner of munitions and equipment to the armed services. So powerful was their influence that it is doubtful if the Japanese could ever have mounted a major war without their backing. It was something of a conundrum as to which came first. Was it the dependence of the military on the munition makers, being the *Zaibatsu*, or did the *Zaibatsu* influence the military in order to aid them in sales and peddling influence? The whole process multiplied as following the success of one supplier the competition followed suit in order to maintain their share of the potential market. The military establishment took over the government, but there is some speculation that the *Zaibatsu* effectively controlled both so that a primary Allied objective following the war was to break up the combines, which will be discussed later.

The launch of a Japanese emergency shipbuilding program and its quick implementation began in 1943, two years after the Ocean class ships were commenced in the US for Britain and the Liberty ship program started. It was also in 1941 that the North Sands Fort and Parks shipbuilding program got underway in Canada. Japan had already shown the world what its young shipbuilding industry could

Hawaii Maru. Osaka Shosen Kaisha (OSK) was the other big Japanese passenger carrier, along with NYK. The company was particularly strong in services to Africa and South America, but generally like its counterpart maintained worldwide services. Here *Hawaii Maru* of 9,450 grt, built in 1915, enters Vancouver Harbour in 1930. If the lifeboats hidden from the camera on the portside match those visible, she carried a total of 20 boats for a large passenger list. (VMM)

do in the First World War by supplying good quality shipping to Britain and the United States. With or without the organizations of the *Zaibatsu* behind them they were to repeat the feat, but this time under far more difficult circumstances.

In the First World War, Japan saw no warfare anywhere near her home islands after the German possessions in North China and the Western Pacific had been taken. She therefore had a clear run in near ideal conditions to produce ships for the Allies and herself and her shipbuilding industry grew enormously. One company, Kawasaki developed a design, as earlier noted, which was repeated so often that it could be termed a standard ship with which Japan equipped herself and other fleets during the wartime period and into the 1920s. In the Second World War, Japan had submarine activity on its sealanes almost from the beginning. The USN's submarine arm was not needed in the European war so, unlike the other branches of its armed forces, the American submarines were able to give their full attention to Japanese shipping from the beginning.

Unlike the British in the Second World War, in most of the rest of the world the Japanese had no readily accessible allies, except for their former enemy, Germany, which with difficulty supplied them with some technical and scientific equipment and information. With its relatively stagnant industries however, Japan was often unable to use this aid to full advantage. One exception to this increasing trend as the war drew to a close was shipbuilding in which the Japanese remained fully on a par with the best in the West. However, they were to all intents and purposes fighting their war unaided and the American submarines inflicted enormous losses on them as US submarine technology improved. As the war progressed, Allied aerial activities increased and British and Dutch submarines based in Australia and Ceylon were able to do much the same, albeit on a smaller scale, throughout the Dutch East Indies and Southeast Asia.

The potential need for wartime shipping was probably apparent to the Japanese government from the beginning. In fact, a retired executive of Ishikawajima-Harima Heavy Industries in Tokyo states that the foundations of a wartime emergency program were laid in 1937. It was also about the time that the British were taking practical steps through their "Scrap and Build" program and the Americans had launched their "C" shipbuilding program to replace obsolete first world war tonnage. Note once again, that critical year of 1937 when tensions in Europe had already grown with the rise of Hitler, and the Italian invasion of Abyssinia, 1935-36. Furthermore the Spanish Civil War was raging over the Iberian Peninsula and engaging Germany and Italy in outright support of the Nationalist movement of Franco, while British, French and Russian interests involved themselves in covert and not-so-covert supply operations to the government side. Everywhere, industry and the man in the street could see that a major war was brewing, even when governments tried to play such notions down.

December 7, 1941 marked the commencement of the Pacific War, but the Japanese did not actually start construction of warbuilt shipping under their emergency program until 1943. Conflict between Japan's navy and army was another reason for delay, as both had their own priorities. They denuded the country's merchant fleet of its best ships for their naval and military purposes and filled the private shipyards with naval work beyond that handled by the navy's own dockyards.

The *Zaibatsu* controlled shipyards—of which Kawaminami, controlled by a minor *Zaibatsu*, was reputed to be the worst—often used many Allied POWs in contravention of the Geneva Convention. The

Zaibatsu controlled shipping concerns took on the biggest share in the ownership of most of the new ships coming out of Japanese yards. NYK alone owned over 20 percent of the Type A, Liberty ship equivalents plus many others from the emergency program.

For the moment it is sufficient to note that the private sector companies actually owned the ships that were allocated to them and, as there was no War Risk insurance coverage, they were entirely on their own in absorbing losses. This subject is dealt with in greater detail in Chapter Three.

Apart from all else, the government was virtually destitute and there was no program such as the Marshall Plan by which the United States assisted in the rebuilding of a devastated Europe from 1948 to 1952. However, there was an advantage to having the MacArthur occupation of Japan as it not only brought resources, but made Japan a valued base for operations when the Korean War broke out in 1950. It also tended to encourage Japan to adopt Douglas MacArthur's own concept of Japanese democracy. Once the economy was recovering and functioning with a sound taxation base, it is evident that incentive schemes in the usual Japanese tradition followed. Such moves included the provision of long term, low interest loans for the building of new ships—all of which favoured Japanese big business which had, through their institutions, an effective tithe on taxation.

It was a different arrangement from that pertaining to Britain, the United States, Canada or Australia, the latter having also initiated its own small wartime emergency program. The Allied governments retained control of all shipping and ownership of most of the wartime tonnage allocating it to the management of private sector owners and then disposing of the ships after the war to their own shipping industries and foreign nationals. Certainly there were no private sector capital interests with the financial strength to take on the ownership of the vast wartime fleets in each country, although some privately owned shipping was built under special license for certain British owners by British yards.

At the end of the war, the Japanese nation was faced with the most shocking devastation accompanied by the near total depletion of its shipping resources; but, in a remarkably short time, the shipbuilding industry was rebuilding facilities, and refurbishing and extending bomb damaged shipyards. The shipyards for the most part escaped the worst effects of American bombing and at war's end about 80 percent of shipbuilding facilities were still operable. They started building new yards once trends to far larger ships became apparent and by the 1950s they were establishing many new overseas connections.

After the war, letters from Japanese trading companies were sent to their old British connections politely sending greetings and asking to re-open connections. There were hints of regret for the recent war and they hoped for business as usual. By and large, that is how international trade was resumed. The truth was, the whole world was starved for normal trade and the victors needed it almost as badly as the vanquished.

By 1952, the ship licensing system was phased out by the US military administration and during the 1950s and 1960s the Japanese trading companies owned by the *Zaibatsu* were opening branch offices in places like Vancouver, Toronto, San Francisco, Seattle, London, and Sydney and many other world trade centres which coincided with their trading interests. Each office embodied many functions. They bought and sold and were ever watchful for good ideas, fresh opportunities, new products, and the provision of services. They also acted as gatherers of market intelligence which covered everything from economic factors, through to assessments of the host country's political and social climate, all of which

Africa Maru. Another passenger carrier of OSK, *Africa Maru*, 9,414 grt, built in 1918, enters Vancouver's Lion's Gate, passing the old Prospect Point lighthouse station. The Lion's Gate Bridge now straddles this point. (VMM)

was fed back to Japan and acted as a guide to research in launching new initiatives. It was an invasion of a different kind and those who had business connections or sought employment opportunities welcomed the Japanese trading companies with open arms and lines of credit from Western banks.

The major shipping companies took hold of the surviving wartime ships of the standard types described in this book and rebuilt some of the inadequately constructed wartime tramps into fast, relatively sleek and efficient cargo liners, oil fired and with their original turbines. These quickly found themselves on the routes to North and South America, Australia and Africa, carrying what little was available in the way of partial cargoes of trade goods most likely to have the greatest appeal to overseas Oriental populations. One ship reopened the NYK service to Europe. At the outset Japanese manufactures for export were virtually unknown as they first had to rebuild their own shattered economy. Even so, the search for raw materials of almost every sort was intense from the beginning and, by the 1950s, Japanese joint ventures with American, Canadian and Australian mining companies were common. They opened up viable deposits of coal, iron, copper and other metals as well as later taking positions in oil, forest products and other forms of manufacturing. They reinvaded the former subjugated countries as traders and investors, but had to deal with the sensitivities of the formerly conquered people with considerable tact. On the whole they made good corporate citizens and their products from television sets to motor cars helped rebuild these other economies.

Today the multiplicity of Japanese connections with major industry are well-established in North and South America, Europe, Asia and Australasia, and are part of the host nation's economy. What could not be obtained by conquest their postwar financial, industrial and trading concerns have developed to the extent that the Japanese economy is linked in thousands of ways to the rest of the Western world. In fact, Japan is the only nation outside of Europe and North America to be a fully accredited member of the G7 countries and is ranked as a full member of the Western nations, in every way except geographically.

Vancouver is typical of hundreds of branch office cities around the world. Here the major trading names like Mitsubishi, Mitsui, Sumitomo, Marubeni, Hitachi, the big carmakers, construction equipment builders and others have been present for upwards of fifty years, forming an important part of our economy. It is little wonder that Japan stands today as the world's second largest industrial economy after the United States.

———————

In the early period immediately after the Second World War, capitalism in totalitarian Germany and Japan was judged to have been heavily involved in the nefarious activities of their countries' political and military machines. In Germany Krupp, Thyssen, I.G. Farbenindustrie and others were found guilty of using slave labour and encouraging or deriving advantage from the criminal research undertaken on political and Jewish prisoners. It was a prime aim of the Allied occupying powers to break the hold that these companies and certain others in the German industrial establishment possessed.

Hikawa Maru, the most famous of a famous trio of popular transpacific diesel liners. Typical of NYK style passenger ships, NYK and OSK were the sole operators of deep sea passenger liners. *Hikawa Maru,* a ship of 11,620 tons was built in 1929 and served as a hospital ship during the war. She is now preserved afloat in Japan. (VMM)

When the occupation of Japan got underway the enormous scope and economic power of the *Zaibatsu* was revealed. Despite all international rules and understandings, their wartime economy was sustained to a remarkable extent by slave and POW labour. Despite this there had been inherent roadblocks of either a philosophical or organizational nature, which meant that a country with the skill to build the world's largest and mightiest battleships—the 68,000 ton *Yamato* and *Musashi*, with the biggest guns ever put to sea—could not take advantage of the superior scientific technology made available by Germany. So far as can be determined the country's aviation industry produced no new worthwhile designs once it had engaged the Allies in war, although no doubt there was much improvement in new versions of existing designs. When Japan did try to catch up, it was too little, too late and from this vantage point the attack on Pearl Harbor, while executed with success by its naval aviators, was one of the biggest misplayed gambles in history. When Admiral Isoruku Yamamoto made his famous remark, "We have awakened a sleeping giant," events were to prove that a truer statement was never made.

By 1945, the ten biggest *Zaibatsu* controlled three quarters of all business, commerce and finance in Japan. It is estimated that the Mitsubishi group's holdings in relative terms were the equivalent of over twenty of the largest American corporations as the market leaders in a range of industries. These included steel, auto manufacturing, oil, non-ferrous metals, aircraft, chemicals, shipbuilding and shipping, heavy equipment, electronics and a dozen other industries.

MacArthur's administration informed the *Zaibatsu* that they would have to disband. This was presented as a voluntary requirement, hence the so-called Yasuda Plan was developed by the *Zaibatsu*, but it was seen by the occupying power as more or less cosmetic. The American administration, following a period of some uncertainty then imposed a plan on the *Zaibatsu* which, while it did not represent a total dispersal of *Zaibatsu* assets, did at least illuminate the dense and complex world of Japanese business. As a result their power was substantially diluted. The top managements of the *Zaibatsu* main companies, their corps of leaders, were dismissed. This affected in particular the Mitsui, Iwasaki (Mitsubishi), Sumitomo families and others who had historically controlled these concerns for the previous hundred years and in some cases, such as Mitsui, for far longer. They were so deeply entrenched in a feudal business system that they could personally see no other alternative.

After the war, *Zaibatsu* families were forced by the MacArthur Administration to part with their companies and most of their lands and properties. The judgement of the Allies was that they had acquiesced and encouraged the military leadership of the country in its wartime adventures. The reasoning followed that these old managements would not be able to cope with a massive redirection and did not deserve a second chance. Their different undertakings were given to employees or tenants in what amounted to a massive redistribution of wealth and the creation of a new, more resilient management class. With a thirst for education, people who would have stood no chance in prewar Japan could now blossom forth with the aid of improved education, and it was within the ranks of these people that the new middle class, which provided most of the postwar managerial function, became firmly rooted. The shipbuilding industry was broken up and reformed, and details of this are included in later chapters.

With the dilution of *Zaibatsu* power there has been a concurrent improvement in the standard of living of the average Japanese which is now closer to, and may well exceed, those in the more advanced Western countries. A large well-educated middle class has grown up and has secured the huge newly formed middle ground between what used to be the feudal lords and the peasantry. The samurai "sword" has been blunted. The expectations of the middle class are influenced by what they see and hear from overseas, for Japanese travel to far distant places on business and on vacations is commonplace. Moreover Japanese investment in other countries and their industries is an important factor in world peace, understanding and the security of ordinary people in the street. Whether they call themselves middle or working class they have expectations in a consumer society that have to be satisfied. This is possibly the best guarantee that a return to Japanese militarism is improbable and that a repeat of its wartime merchant shipping program, certainly the hastiest of any in the last or any other war, will never be repeated. This also heightens the uniqueness of the Japanese wartime standard ships among all their wartime contemporaries.

Interestingly enough, as the naked power of the *Zaibatsu* has declined as a percentage of the overall Japanese economy, the postwar rise of their equivalent in Korea has been noteworthy. Called *Chaebol* by the Koreans, the giant conglomerates Hyundai, Samsung and Daewoo have, like many of the *Zaibatsu* become household names among world industrial undertakings, building everything from ships to automobiles and television sets. They have become well known through familiar brand names for manufactured products. Unlike the Japanese who built on enormous corporate resources, Korean growth has been founded on high leverage and heavy debt financing to make up for its late start on the world scene. Much of this has been at the heart of the financial crisis that hit Korea and spread throughout the Far East during the 1990s, undermining several economies including that of Japan.

CHAPTER TWO

THE FIRST JAPANESE WAR LOSS: EVENTS PRECEDING PEARL HARBOR

ONE DETAIL OF THE PERIOD between the outbreak of the war in Europe and the Pacific War concerns a specific ship. This vessel was *Terukuni Maru*, which with her sister, *Yasukuni Maru*, was employed on the Japan-Northern Europe route of the NYK, referred to by the Japanese as the "Europe Line." This service was really split in two with larger, faster passenger freighters calling at Hamburg, Antwerp, and London with liberty to call at Middlesborough, if there was sufficient cargo there to make a stop worthwhile.

This was a twice monthly service, but in addition there were once monthly freighter services calling at Hamburg, Bremen, Rotterdam and Antwerp, which were called the "North Continental Service" and, quite separately, the "West Coast Service" calling at the British ports of Newport, Swansea, Glasgow and Birkenhead. In total this was an important route for NYK on which it competed with Blue Funnel, Ellerman, Ben Line and P&O among the British companies, plus several continental lines including

Norddeutscher Lloyd, Rickmers, Wilhelmsen, the Danish and Swedish East Asiatic companies, as well as Italian and French lines.

In addition NYK acted as European agents for OSK which operated a service direct from Japanese and North China ports, to San Francisco, New York via Panama, thence to Antwerp, Rotterdam, Bremen and Hamburg. Kawasaki KK ships were also prominent in the tramp trades. Their ships were regular visitors to Fowey in the southwest of England where they loaded substantial cargoes of the locally produced kaolin clay, reputed to be the best in the world for the manufacture of ceramics and the famous Japanese porcelain.

All of this important trade was shattered on November 2, 1939, when *Terukuni Maru* was sunk by a magnetic mine off Harwich on the East Coast of England. She was the only Japanese war casualty outside of East Asia, prior to the attack on Pearl Harbor. She was a valuable motorship, built with her sister in 1930. As a passenger/cargo liner of 11,931 gross registered tons with a deadweight capacity of 10,155 tons, she had a speed of almost 18 knots but usually ran at 15.30 knots, according to NYK. She was of the type that would have made a first class army transport or would have been pressed into naval or hospital service in the event of war.

Terukuni Maru was lost near the Sunk Lightship at 51.50.4N, 01.31.04E. She carried a crew of 177 and 28 passengers and had a mixed cargo of regular trade goods such as sardines, ochre, gum arabic, camphor and coconut. She went down in twenty minutes, but not before Captain Matsukura had managed to beach her on the Shipwash sand where she rested on her side in eight fathoms. There was no loss of life.

By 1939, Japan and Germany had developed a close alliance, so it was with some degree of cynicism that the British news reports drily noted that the Japanese government had lodged a strong protest with Berlin; but, if this one event had any bearing on the Axis Alliance, it was not in any way apparent. The NYK history, *Voyage of a Century* (Tokyo, 1985) perhaps with tongue in cheek notes: "As neither side would admit to the mine being theirs, no compensation was obtained," for the loss of their ship.

Typically the Japanese government expected the total dedication of its private and corporate citizens to its purposes, but shipowners were on their own when it came to War Risks insurance. It was also inconceivable that the British would have laid sophisticated magnetic mines in their own shipping lanes and, apart from the fact that the magnetic mine was a German invention, it is not certain that the magnetic mine was ever adopted by the British or Americans.

To say the least this was a very diplomatic statement on the part of NYK that was calculated to offend no one. For those of us who were closer to hand and remember the German magnetic mine campaign by which the Thames estuary and much of the English coast was liberally sown with this early secret weapon of the war, there was never any doubt as to who "owned" the mine. German aircraft had dropped the mines by parachute. The German magnetic mines were highly effective until degaussing gear was installed in Allied ships; until then, losses were very heavy.

The Salvage Association, London, was called in to examine the wreck, probably on instructions from NYK. They concluded that even though much of the port side was exposed and entry could have been gained by cutting holes in her side, it meant cutting away her upperworks to right her. Apart from all else, with British, German and French yards fully occupied with national war work, no one was theo-

Terukuni Maru. Two photos that show this first class
motor passenger-cargo liner, which with her sister ship
Yasukuni Maru, was employed in NYK's Japan-Europe
Line. Built in 1930, of 11,000 grt, *Terukuni Maru* had
the unique distinction of being the only Japanese war loss
in the Second World War prior to the Pearl Harbor
attack, when she was mined off England's east coast.
(NYK)

Terukuni Maru. Seen here lying abandoned on a sandbank
off Harwich, England. She was neutral property when
fatally holed by a German magnetic mine in 1939. She
became enemy property after December 7, 1941. No
attempt was made to salvage the ship, as she lay on her
side. In 1946 the remains were blown up by the British as
part of the program to remove wartime wrecks. (NYK)

Suwa Maru. The last Japanese ship to leave European waters when Japan recalled all its shipping following the Allied embargo on raw material exports to Japan after her seizure of Indo-China in mid-1941. *Suwa Maru* of 10,700 grt was built in Japan in 1914 and is a good example of the capability of Japanese shipbuilders in that era. (NYK)

Nippon Maru. In the 1930s the Japanese government encouraged private owners to build a number of fast motor tankers in the range of 15,000 deadweight tons, with a speed of up to 18 knots. These were employed in bringing in cargoes of California and Texas crude oil to build up Imperial Japanese Navy fuel reserves. This ship was the only tanker owned by Yamashita Kisen KK when war broke out in Europe in 1939. (Mitsubishi)

retically in a position to raise her and there was nowhere she could have been taken for repair. The only possibility was a Dutch salvage concern such as Smit or Wijsmuller and a Dutch repair yard.

At the time of her loss, she was neutral property and remained so for any purpose involving salvage. It is likely however, that she would have been raised after Japan entered the war had it been worthwhile for the British to do so; but two years were to elapse before that could happen, by which time exposure to sea and weather would have taken their toll. Thus the ship, which remained on her starboard side on the sandbank, would have likely been at least partly swallowed by the sand. There is no indication that she constituted a hazard to navigation, which would have justified removal of the wreck. At the time the main shipping channel off the East coast was littered with wrecks sunk by German mines and aircraft.

In 1946, the British demolished *Terukuni Maru* with explosives in an effort to clean up war debris.

There is a feature of Japanese merchant shipping about which I have seen no official or other, speculative comment. This concerns the position of Japanese ships in foreign harbours or at sea when the Pacific War commenced. If there were instances of Japanese ships being interned, captured at sea or scuttled, I can find no reference to such events, as none ever seem to have taken place.

In fact, in the large fleet of former German and Italian ships which were operated for the British Ministry of War Transport, which had been given "Empire" names and were listed in Mitchell and Sawyer's book *Empire Ships of World War II*, there is a notable absence of any former Japanese vessels prior to 1945. The handful of small vessels which were incorporated into the British merchant fleet were obviously postwar seizures taken in Southeast Asia. In a similar way, a limited number of smaller ships might have also been seized by the Americans, particularly in the Philippines and elsewhere.

However, during 1941 it is hardly credible that a massive quantity of Japanese shipping could be simply withdrawn without it's being noticed, but this is more or less what appeared to happen. No doubt the professional shipping press noticed it from its beginning but, at least in Britain and probably in Canada and the United States, the popular press made little, if any, reference to the disappearance of Japanese shipping from the high seas and its accumulation in its home ports in Japan. Changes in shipping patterns and trade movements are quickly noted in a variety of ways through reports from many sources such as commodity traders and their markets, shipping agents, Lloyd's agents, insurance and banking people engaged in trade transactions.

Following the seizure of French Indo-China in July 1941, the alarm bells rang throughout the Far East, Southeast Asia and the West. Japanese expansionist ambitions were obvious. The Dutch East Indies, Australia and New Zealand were alarmed as was India, which was aware of the vulnerability of its long east coast and its frontier with Burma. All took comfort in supposedly impregnable Singapore and the strength of the Royal Navy. However, Britain was already fully occupied in the North Atlantic and Mediterranean when Pearl Harbor occurred and two vigorous years of war at sea had thinned her resources. Moreover, Britain knew all along that Singapore was not impregnable and that a secret Admiralty assessment to this effect which had fallen into the hands of the Germans was passed to the Japanese. This document probably gave the overly ambitious gamblers in Tokyo great comfort in their plans for conquest. In addition the American mobilization of its human, technical and material resources was a long way from being fully implemented.

The United States had embargoed sales of California and Texas crude oil to Japan in July 1941, which forced the Japanese to look elsewhere for their supplies. This was the immediate result of the French Indo-China invasion. The Miri oilfield in Brunei, North Borneo was the closest, operated by Royal Dutch Shell, which also occupied a key position in the Dutch East Indies oil industry based in Java, Sumatra and Borneo. Beyond these locations were the Burmah Oil company holdings in British-controlled Burma but there was no development of the large Chinese or Indonesian offshore oil resources. Both were to be developed long after the war was over. The only fuel in which Japan was partly self-sufficient was relatively low grade coal that she supplemented with Manchurian coal. Coal was a major factor in the Japanese industrial economy, but its thrust to the south only gained Japan the Chinese coal field on the island of Hainan with its port at Haiphong.

Britain, the Commonwealth nations and the Dutch in the Netherlands East Indies followed a similar policy as the US in a probably useless effort to head off Japanese aggression by adopting trade sanctions leading to economic strangulation. The West probably felt that Japan's activities in China had already stretched its resources to a breaking point, but if so it was an underestimation of Japanese strength and resolve. Also, Japanese concepts of honour would not allow them to be humbled. At the time of Pearl Harbor, Japanese emissaries were negotiating a peaceful compromise in Washington and it appears that the two civilian representatives concerned were genuine enough, as they represented the Peace Party in Japan. On the other hand General Hideki Tojo and his supporters were thirsting for war and it is doubtful that anything short of an intercession from the Emperor Hirohito would have stopped them.

Steel scrap was a commodity which Japan purchased in huge quantities for its steel smelters. A high proportion of this material came from the United States and this was also embargoed prior to Pearl Harbor. Unlike oil however, this might have been seen as a less hostile act. It was also evidence of a mounting demand for the metal within the United States as it increased production of all types of steel, in particular shipbuilding steel, some of which it also supplied to Canada and Britain.

By the time of Pearl Harbor, a massive shipbuilding effort was well under way in the United States and Canada which would augment and eventually overtake Britain's wartime effort in building merchant ships. Like Japan and the United States, Britain also had a large warship program constantly underway, but unlike Japan it included a huge effort to build fleets of escort vessels, to which Canada also made a massive contribution. The two countries between them built many hundreds of escorts, including the ubiquitous corvettes and the more powerful frigates.

The embargo was such that for Japan to accept it meant economic strangulation. Sooner or later however, that would lead to war as Japan could not function for long without the stimulus of readily obtained natural resources. The Americans, British and Dutch were aware of this, and in spite of claims to the contrary the attack when it came was probably anticipated in some form. Pearl Harbor might not have been the complete surprise that President Roosevelt talked of in his famous "Day of Infamy" speech following the attack. In fact, the British had warned the Americans of impending attack after they had penetrated the Japanese code. Interestingly, such an attack was the one thing that would swing American public opinion firmly behind the war effort.

Events in Japan leading to war had been moving ahead for some time. The power of the pro-war militarists had been growing since the 1920s so that, by the time of the attack on China in 1934, the militarists were firmly in power. General Tojo was war minister in the late 1930s. As such he was in charge of expanding the Japanese Armed Forces. With Pearl Harbor approaching, he was appointed prime minister which gave him great power. No one in the senior ranks was more in favour of war than Tojo and with that kind of power it should come as no surprise that the army dominated the navy in joint staff deliberations. The name of Tojo joined the Allied rogues' gallery along with Hitler and Mussolini.

With the embargo in place there was little chance of Japanese shipping being caught in an endangered position. From July, the month of the march into Indo-China, to December 7 the Japanese had adequate time to work their shipping back into home waters. The Japanese military and naval authorities had sufficient time and the broadest possible choice in preparing their ships as military transports and other purposes as necessary. Converting merchant ships into military or naval auxiliaries, such as seaplane carriers or attack transports, with elaborate special equipment and power requirements could not be undertaken on short notice or without considerable planning.

When Pearl Harbor was attacked, Japanese convoys laden with munitions and troops were already underway to attack Hong Kong, the Philippines, Malaya, Singapore and the Indies. Again, preparations on this scale must have been made far earlier so that, when Allied sanctions were imposed in July 1941, they may have begun to inconvenience the Japanese economy but they also played right into the hands of the military hierarchy. The assault, when it came, was massive and well prepared and could be said to have commenced when Admiral Yamamoto issued his famous coded order to launch the Pearl Harbor assault, "*Niitaka yama no bore*," which meant "Ascend Mount Niitaka."

The Japanese Navy struck with a ferocity and efficiency that crushed all before it. The army seemed to mesmerize the usually weak Allied defences. With the exception of MacArthur's defence of Bataan and Corregidor in the Philippines and, the British rearguard action in Malaya which delayed the fall of Singapore by about two months, the rest collapsed with incredible speed in the face of the Japanese onslaught. The most appalling defeat was that of the British at Singapore. Ballyhooed in the media as an impregnable fortress, it was the keystone of British power and defences throughout the Far East, but its heavy guns were trained to seaward and could not be brought to bear on the landward attack from the rear when it came. Such a mistake, when viewed retrospectively, now seems incredible given that some better planning in the construction stage would have recognised that danger. The wave of Japanese invasion came to a stop with the Australians in New Guinea, the Americans in the Solomons and the British at the back door to India in Assam and Manipur.

Japan's hurried conquest of much of the Far East and Southeast Asia was viewed in much the same way as society sees an armed robbery. The robber comes in behind the muzzle of a gun and takes whatever he wants. This appeared to the rest of the world as a barefaced grab for land and the resources that went with it, and the enslavement of civilian populations in the interests of manpower. It was robbery with violence on the grandest scale imaginable. The Japanese leadership ignored the heavy censure of the rest of the world and, for its newly conquered empire propagandized the term, the "Greater East Asia Co-Prosperity Sphere."

None of the subjugated peoples shared in this co-prosperity and even Japan's own people were called upon to make incredible sacrifices and tasted few if any of the fruits of victory. The Allies, at first militarily weak, soon marshalled a stronger resistance and, as they gradually built their strength, ultimately gave the Japanese a lesson they would never forget.

Japanese Submarine *I-23*. Submarines of the Imperial
Japanese Navy had a long range, patrolling as far west as
the Red Sea, South Africa and across the Pacific to the
west coast of Canada and the United States. While they
were employed aggressively they did not enjoy the success
ratios of their German allies or American opponents.
(Japan Archives)

CHAPTER THREE

THE PROSECUTION OF THE PACIFIC WAR

AT THE TIME OF PEARL HARBOR THE JAPANESE MERCHANT MARINE was at a peacetime peak. Figures from the Japanese Ministry of Transport indicate it numbered 1,581 steamships of 4.1 million gross tons and 756 motorvessels of 1.5 million gross tons for a total of 5.6 million gross tons. In addition, a large fleet of wooden trading and fishing sailing vessels totalling some 17,992 units, of an estimated 1.07 million gross tons were also on the Japanese register. According to the NYK history, the Japanese war effort resulted in the total tonnage growing to 9,950,000 gross tons but of this grand total, 85 percent was lost so that barely 1.5 million tons remained at the end of the war. It was a mere fraction of the country's needs in either peace or war. The increase would be accounted for by the ships added through the emergency programs and a small amount of captured Allied tonnage, mostly Chinese, Hong Kong, Philippines, East Indies and Singapore small-tonnage ships. A few larger Allied ships were also captured in damaged condition following bombing along with three Empire-type standard tramps under construction for the British government at the time of the capture of Hong Kong.

The Japanese powered vessels followed European practice and design and, while the number would have included a variety of ferries and harbour service craft, one could estimate (using a factor of gross tons x 1.45) that 5.6 million gross tons might have an overall deadweight capacity of about 8.12 million tons. Outside of Europe and the United States it represented a powerful and strategically well-placed fleet. The sailing vessels were for the most part coastal craft used in the short sea trades, and

Opposite top: Seaplane Carrier *Kimikawa*. Typical of the best ships in Japan's merchant marine, Kawasaki Lines' *Kimikawa Maru* was ready for Japan's aggressive thrust into Southeast Asia and the Pacific Islands. The third set of kingposts between numbers 4 and 5 hatches was removed, and a powerful catapult installed in its place. With most of the best ships taken over by the army and navy, the merchant marine was left with a high proportion of steam tramp tonnage of First World War vintage. (Japan Archives)

Opposite middle: Convoy Underway. Some of the earliest convoys destined to invade the Philippines, Hong Kong and points south were underway before the attack on Pearl Harbor. Here a Japanese convoy column is underway for points unknown. Other columns are probably to the right, out of sight of the camera. (Japan Archives)

Opposite bottom: An Escort Vessel. The Imperial Navy started the war with a critical deficiency in escort vessels which was never corrected. That, and inadequate anti-submarine warfare tactics, were among the reasons Japanese sinkings and crew losses were so high. (Japan Archives)

with few exceptions they followed traditional Japanese practice and constituted an important economic element in the country's commerce.

The West was familiar with the quality of Japanese shipbuilding, as a number of new freighters were built in Japan during the First World War for the British and Americans. The British ships were flushdecked, tramp-type steam-powered freighters of about 9,000 dwt, typical of much of the tonnage in the NYK fleet. NYK as the leading Japanese company might have played an intermediary role in negotiating the shipbuilding contracts. After the war these ships were sold off to civilian operators such as Messageries Maritimes of Paris, France and the Larrinaga Steamship Company of Liverpool. They gave good service for a normal ship life of some twenty-four years.

A larger type ship was built for the United States government account which was bigger than all the standard ships that came off the building ways in the US, with the exception of the Hog Island passenger ships operated by United States Lines. Altogether the Americans placed orders in Japanese yards for forty-five vessels, the largest being the group with a tonnage of 8,150 gross registered tons and an estimated deadweight tonnage of up to 12,000 tons. They were of American design with six full-size hatches and machinery amidships, and they gave a hint of the C3- type ships which first came out in the late 1930s.

Two of them found their way into the Luckenbach Steam Ship Company fleet and gave an excellent account of themselves in the intercoastal lumber trade in the interwar years. When built they exceeded their designed speed by an unheard-of four knots which evidently more than satisfied their new owners. On account of their speed and size, they made good emigrant passenger/cargo liners when converted to this purpose by the Costa Line of Italy following the Second World War.

The First World War proved that Japan was an emerging economic and industrial giant. The first dreadnoughts for the Japanese Navy were built in Britain, but by 1911 all future battleships and cruisers and other naval vessels were to come from Japanese yards and Japanese designs. By the end of the First World War and throughout the 1920s and 1930s, they were able to match anything in the way of warships built in Europe and America. The fleet included some of the largest aircraft carriers and a powerful array of fast, eight-inch-gunned heavy cruisers which played a major role in overcoming the smaller, more lightly armed cruisers of the Allied navies. One example is the total destruction of a combined British, American, Australian and Dutch fleet of cruisers and destroyers at the battle of the Java Sea. As noted previously, before the war ended Japan had built and lost the two largest battleships ever built, the *Yamato* and *Musashi*. The Yamato class battleships were incredible ships, the like of which the

Destroyer Type. The Imperial Navy did have a large fleet of destroyers, many of them heavy units and all fast and generally efficient, which were usually employed on fleet duties escorting heavier ships. They also had a small number rated as torpedo boats or light destroyers. These were of similar size to a US destroyer escort. The ship illustrated here appears to be an Otori class vessel. (Japan Archives)

Japanese Heavy Cruisers. Fast and powerful, usually with more guns than comparable ships of the Allied navies, the heavy cruisers were a decisive element in the war of aggression. It was a heavy cruiser group that annihilated the joint Dutch-British-Australian-US fleet in one of the earliest engagements of the Pacific war, the battle of the Java Sea. The ship illustrated was similar in appearance to *Haguro*, *Myoko* and *Takao*, mentioned in the text. (Japan Archives)

The Wreck of a Cruiser. A casualty of the Java Sea battle.
Believed to be the wreck of the Dutch cruiser *Java*, sunk
by Japanese forces on January 27 1942, somewhere near
Sourabaya, the main Dutch naval base on the island of
Java. (Wm. Hutcherson)

world's navies had never seen before and will certainly never see again. They were bigger and technically more powerful than the biggest and best in any of the world's other navies. Some idea of their colossal size and power is conveyed from the following vital statistics. A third ship was completed as the aircraft carrier *Shinano*, but she was lost on her delivery voyage. The fourth of the class was dismantled where she lay after the war.

Yamato Class
Displacement tonnage: 62,315 tons; 69,900 tons fully laden
Length overall: 840 feet
Breadth: 121 feet
Draft: 34 feet
Shaft Horsepower: 150,000
Speed: 27 knots
Main Guns: 9 x 18.2 inch
Armour: 16" belt

In retrospect, the building of such huge ships now seems to have been a waste of scarce resources, but prior to the aircraft carrier becoming dominant it was typical naval thinking that one country's latest class of battleships, cruisers or destroyers always seem to call for a "reply" from a potential opponent. It implied that the planners, at least on paper, were always engaged in thinking of the next war at the planning level. Realistically however, it was part of the escalating arms race which led up to both world wars. In Japanese naval circles it seems reasonable to suppose that the Yamatos were built in response to the latest American battleships of the Iowa class or vice versa.

Yamato. With her sister, *Musashi*, they were the greatest battleships ever built with the biggest dimensions and firepower. The Japanese people even to this day have considerable pride in their construction, but these giants represented an enormous drain on the national treasury and industrial resources without any significant effect on the outcome of the war. (Japan Archives)

During the 1930s, a high proportion of new Japanese ships were fast diesel freighters and tankers which provided a ready pool of naval auxiliaries when the war came, although this quickly shrank in the face of war losses. The Japanese believed in speed, so with new tankers and cargo liners an operating speed of 16 to 19 knots was common at a time when 12 knots was favoured by the West and 14 knots was regarded as fast in these classes. The buildup of the country's merchant navy was also augmented by steady purchases of foreign secondhand shipping, much of it British and Canadian first world war construction of generally good quality. Among these ships were some examples of British fully prefabricated, N type freighters, which are believed by the author to have played a part in the development of the Japanese Type A ship that is a primary subject of this book. (See Chapter Six).

Following Pearl Harbor the Japanese Empire expanded over a massive area which took it to the gates of Australia and India. As noted earlier, the one arm of the Allied forces which was able to react quickly was the US Navy submarine fleet which promptly started a campaign against Japanese shipping. Results were poor at first because of flaws in American torpedoes, but ultimately they were every bit as effective as the German Kriegsmarine could bring to bear in the North Atlantic. The Dutch navy had a small flotilla of submarines stationed in the East Indies when Japan attacked. The Dutch surface ships were decimated but their submarines enjoyed success against the invading fleet. Most escaped and fought the rest of the war as part of a British/Dutch submarine fleet based in Australia.

It was obvious that, as the Japanese tide of conquest spread itself through the Western Pacific and Southeast Asia, it also carried the seeds of its own ultimate destruction as supply lines became longer and more exposed to attack from a more powerful enemy. Submarine penetration in fact soon proved that the porous boundaries of the new Japanese empire were virtually indefensible.

However, the wartime program came nowhere near the volume of shipping built in the United States, Britain and Canada, whose combined war machines turned out the ships and munitions which eventually swamped the enemy. Moreover, and most critically, the Allies built a large accompanying fleet of escorts, so while there was seldom the number of escort ships to give the protection convoy commanders would have liked, both the number and quality of escorts and light carriers with air cover potential was superior to anything the Axis navies could provide. This was particularly true with the Japanese who had to cover enormous distances in their far-flung empire. *Jane's Fighting Ships* at the end of the war readily indicated the deficiency in suitable light escort ships which were equivalent to American destroyer escorts or British and Canadian frigates and corvettes.

By nature the Japanese are a courageous people and there is little doubt there were plenty of heroes among their merchant sailors. The reality was that 62,692 Japanese merchant marine personnel lost their lives according to official government estimates originating in Japan. That almost equals the 62,923 from the British Commonwealth, the United States and Allied countries with a significant merchant marine, except Russian or Chinese losses at sea, according to British and Allied official government figures.

This suggests that Japanese escort and rescue services were at a minimum and bears out the position that Japan consistently neglected to provide more escort vessels rather than putting resources into giant battleships. A small number of medium-sized merchant ships were converted to escort-type carriers but there appears to have been no evidence of them being used in convoy protection duties. Correspondence with R.J. Tompkins of Australia suggests that convoys were often unescorted and had to make a dash from one Japanese controlled port to another during the hours of darkness. While awaiting the next stage of the journey, they would lay over during daylight hours, and often became sitting ducks for Allied planes, particularly as the war approached its end. Not only did the failure to provide adequate escorts increase ship losses, but without escorts any hope of crews being rescued once pitched into the sea was minimal and added to the toll in human life.

In general, Japanese crews declined to be picked up by Allied ships or submarines. The sense of honour which guided them in their oath of loyalty and devotion to the Emperor were such that it was a disgrace to be picked up and taken prisoner. It was far better to go to their deaths than to become prisoners, which was one reason why brutality towards Allied prisoners was so common. It was a matter of holding POWs in contempt. Their values held that it was far better that they should die with honour on the field of battle and they evidently thought their opponents should hold the same values.

––––––––––––––

Research for this book produced some challenges when comparisons were made with, on the one hand, practices applying to War Risks insurance and on the other the methodology involved in managing and owning Japanese merchant tonnage built as part of that country's emergency standard shipbuilding program.

In peacetime, War Risks insurance is provided by the private sector marine insurance underwriters as an available coverage for H&M (hull and machinery) and cargo at a rate which reflects the level of risk. A good example concerned British shipping running the Franco blockade during the Spanish Civil War, 1936-39. The risks of capture, seizure and the consequences of warlike activity ranged from moderate to extremely high, and the rates went through the roof when exposure to risk was extreme. No commercial venture could have paid the rates required unless the main beneficiary—in this case the Spanish government out of sheer necessity—could have covered the cost out of funds it held on deposit in London. Although the need for war risks insurance arose because of a war, Britain itself was at peace, so the risks of war remained covered in the private market.

When Britain went to war in 1939, one of the first acts of the British government was to take over war risks on all hulls and cargo sailing to and from Britain or acting under government order, but cross-voyages, such as the annual tea crop from India to the United States, was covered by the private market for cargo risks. Likewise, when all shipping was placed under government direction, the war risk to hulls, privately and government-owned, was assumed by the British government. Compensation for privately owned shipping when lost by act of war, was supposedly carried to a special account held for the private owner and then recovered after the war by a cash settlement or by a transfer of title to government-owned shipping of equivalent value.

Practical day-to-day management of shipping remained with the private owners of their ships, although they were always subject to government direction of actual employment. British government owned ships or ships taken on bareboat charter from the Dominion of Canada or Lend-Lease from the United States War Shipping Administration and placed on the British register were allocated under management contracts to specified private owners and shown in the ownership description of the ship in

Assault Transport. A combination of amphibious landing craft and fast transport. There were 26 of the class built. They were propelled by turbines with a speed of 16 knots and displacement of 1,129 tons. Most were operated by the Japanese Army and were used for fast transfers of troops and supplies. (Japan Archives)

Lloyd's Register, the war risks being fully assumed by the British government.

Canadian vessels in Canadian operational control were registered to Park Steamship Company, a crown agency and likewise allocated to private managers; but unlike British practice no mention of managers appeared in Lloyd's Register, or the National Shipping List. Again, the War Risks on such vessels were assumed by the Canadian government.

The United States retained title to its shipping through its agencies, the US War Shipping Administration, or the United States Maritime Commission, but whatever methods applied in each of the three countries there was no doubt as to legal ownership of government-owned property and the fact that War Risks were assumed by the government in question. The investment in government-owned ships and armaments generally was made out of revenue or reserves and, when lost, the loss became a direct charge against that revenue or reserves. Government War Risks insurance was therefore represented by an accounting exercise rather than a policy of insurance as would apply to private sector insurance.

The process of compensating private owners was dependent on one key element—ultimate victory. Had the Western Allies been defeated there would have almost certainly been no form of compensation. A similar situation prevailed in Japan. In that country, the promise was made that shipowners would be compensated for war losses following Japan's victory, but as that victory never happened the promise could not be kept, so there was no compensation as such. In defeat the nation was impoverished and the government could do nothing to uphold promises made by the wartime administration.

However, it was in the manner in which title to wartime emergency ships was handled that a clear distinction existed between Japanese practice and the processes employed by the Western Allies. The administration and planning of wartime shipping was allocated to the Imperial Japanese Navy and the actual financing of shipbuilding was a government function, which it evidently handled by requiring the

Wooden Vessels. To help with the shortfall in shipping, the Japanese initiated an ambitious wooden vessel construction program. This small armed vessel is believed to be an example. (Japan Archives)

The death of a ship, near Amoy in 1945. A Japanese escort type ship
succumbs to aerial attack from an American B-25 bomber in this
sequence of photographs. Survivors fight for their lives either in sliding
down the ship's side, or swimming alongside. (US Army Air Force)

Japanese shipping companies to actually purchase the ships as they were completed and legally incorporate them as owned units for manning by their own crews.

At the commencement of the Pacific War, the private shipping companies possessed financial reserves accumulated out of their normal trading operations, but it seems probable that the government wanted to marshal these reserves to its own ends. Without exercising some form of confiscatory taxation, the government appears to have raided these reserves by requiring the private shipping companies to purchase the ships. This relieved the government of the burden of financial ownership while it retained full operating control as it did for all other shipping. For the government it was a matter of financing its obligations with someone else's money and allowing them no say in the control of the asset. These wartime ships were held in low regard by the shipping companies on account of their design and structural limitations, which fell far below fully classed ships. They assumed ownership, undoubtedly with many misgivings, because they were ordered to do so with only a vague promise of compensation for war losses if Japan won the war.

Management of these wartime ships was conducted by a *Senpaku Un'eikei* (Shipping Operation Board), which was an organization set up by representatives of major shipping companies for the ships serving civilian needs. When requisitioned by the military, management was taken over and directed by the transportation headquarters of the army and navy. Given the state of conflict that often arose between these two branches of the services, management must have been very complicated indeed.

The Japanese clearly went further than the Western Allies in forcing the obligations of ownership on their private citizens in this manner. With defeat came the inevitable consequence that the shipping companies were nearly prostrate. The shipbuilding companies at least had possession of their lands and only a depletion of the productive assets through Allied bombing. Most of the country's merchant fleet had been lost and corporate reserves were severely depleted so that companies from NYK down were faced with enormous challenges in the absence of compensation. Effectively, they had to start from the beginning and the only way in which they could be offered help from government sources depended on the rebuilding process and how the future would unfold for a resurgent Japan.

A device developed by the Japanese securities market, very soon after the war was to seek foreign participation in its stock market by way of a "letter of authority." This enabled securities companies to buy shares on behalf of foreign clients and hold them on their behalf as nominees. This got around an embargo on direct foreign investment in Japanese securities. This was tried in 1952 by advertising in foreign financial journals. Receipt of a detailed summary of all Japanese shipping stocks is well-remembered and it was hoped that through this device some activity could be generated into an otherwise stagnant stock market. It was part of the process of rebuilding.

As government reserves and revenue slowly climbed Japan did what it had always done in the past. It provided laws favourable to rebuilding privately owned shipping fleets and with them a package of government-guaranteed, low-cost and extended finance. Interest was subsidized, but was required to be repaid later when conditions had normalized.

This was in line with the historical record going back to the Meiji Restoration. Japan, more than almost all other countries, had shaped its merchant marine to its basic trading needs, its political ends, and as an instrument of action and necessity in peace and war.

An early casualty of the war. This wreck appears to have been a Kawasaki "stock boat" or similar. She was lying close by the wreck of the Dutch cruiser *Java*. The picture was taken from the Canadian ship *Weston Park*, heading into Javanese waters after the war. (Wm. Hutcherson)

CHAPTER FOUR

THE COLLAPSE OF AN EMPIRE AND PERSONAL MEMORIES

THE ARM OF THE JAPANESE NAVY that distinguished itself the least in Allied eyes was their submarine service. In the book *A Great Fleet of Ships: Canada's Forts and Parks*, the story is told of the loss of the British- flagged, Canadian-built and American-owned *Fort Mumford* at the hands of Commander Fukumura and his submarine *I 27*. Fukumura machine-gunned the *Mumford* survivors, leaving just one alive to tell of the atrocity. This followed a similar atrocity involving the British-flag Liberty ship *Sambridge*. The British, soon after the *Fort Mumford* incident, wreaked vengeance on Fukumura when he attacked a small troop convoy in the Indian Ocean, sinking the liner *Khedive Ismail* with heavy loss of life. Fukumura's submarine took refuge under the large number of survivors in the water, but that did not prevent the escorts from depth-charging him and bringing his sub to the surface to be destroyed. The death toll among the merchant survivors was very heavy, but all the Japanese crew of the sub perished. This contrasted so sharply with German Kapitänleutnant Robert Gysae's attack in *U 177* on the Canadian-flag *Jasper Park* in the same general area, which was detailed in the same book. The German submariners were not noted for compassion, but it was seldom they stepped beyond acceptable international behaviour. (Let it also be noted that British and American submarine commanders as well,

Top: Assault Transport. This type of combination amphibious landing craft and fast transport was illustrated in the previous chapter. This photo of one of the class on fire is believed to have been taken in the Philippines, one of the areas where the type was generally employed. The others were Japan and Korea. (US Official)

Bottom: Stranded wreck. This wreck has been beached in a shallow bay, possibly in the Philippines. Fire has gutted the upperworks and the hold ahead of the bridge, where the shell plating appears to have buckled under the intense heat of the fire. (US Official)

quickly learned despite international conventions that torpedoing without warning gave them a better chance of survival.)

Japan is estimated to have lost 125 submarines during the war, most of them to American anti-submarine attacks. According to figures calculated from the first postwar edition of *Jane's Fighting Ships*, from an initial 80 subs, 71 were added through new construction and Japan ended the war with 26 operational subs, a far higher loss ratio than either of the American or British submarine fleets. Japanese survivors of submarine sinkings were usually few as most declined to be picked up by Allied submarines if the rare opportunity arose. The Japanese believed in dying with their boats, and accounts of interrogated submariners are equally rare. Such may exist, but I have found none of an anecdotal nature in my research.

The US Navy also had a large fleet of submarines at its disposal and these were deployed almost before any other offensive activity could be undertaken by the Americans. Moreover, they had already adopted the same economies through standardization as the *Kriegsmarine* and, like the latter service with its heavy reliance on the Type VII, American submarine builders turned strongly to standard designs.

A factor of great concern to the US Navy at the outset of the war was the unreliability of its torpedoes to the extent that a number of attacks on the enemy were frustrated. This contrasted badly with the Japanese "Long Lance" torpedo, reputed to be one of the success stories of the war.

Grand Admiral Karl Dönitz's achievement in building the German submarine arm stands out above all others, but the rival American dedication to a single class constructed with economy and efficiency in mind is also noteworthy. With this fleet and its prewar boats, the Americans conducted a war of attrition against the Japanese merchant navy which rivalled the German effort in the North Atlantic. Unlike the Allies, as earlier noted, the Japanese Navy was chronically short of escort vessels, but their destroyers were fast and deadly.

The late Commander W. Kinsman RCN (Rtd), gave an account in his personal memoir, *Before I Forget*, of his service with the RN in the British S and T class submarines, of which many in both classes were deployed against Japanese shipping in Southeast Asian waters. Kinsman served in the submarine *Thorough*. He relates that the British submarines based on Fremantle, Western Australia, had considerable difficulty in finding worthwhile targets particularly once the Japanese retreat got underway. What the Japanese had not withdrawn from the area, in the way of larger deep-draught vessels had already been sunk. As they were able, large merchant ships and warships were withdrawn by the Japanese generally to home waters, which more or less meant those waters to the north of Luzon and Formosa Straits, which were the North Pacific entrances to the South China Sea.

Kinsman complained of the shortage of targets, most of which his boat disposed of by shellfire as they hardly merited a torpedo, being small vessels. The British submarines were withdrawn to Fremantle or Trincomalee in Ceylon to make way for the retaking of Malaya and on the way in the invasion force passed some of them coming across the Bay of Bengal in the approach to the Straits of Malacca.

Despite heavy bombing of Japanese mainland cities and industrial installations, most of the important shipyards survived, relatively speaking, in better shape than many of the other industrial and military undertakings. The fact that only about 20 percent of productive shipyard facilities were put out of

Another beached wreck. The debris of war litters the foreground, while this freighter awaits removal. She appears to be fire damaged and salvageable, probably from a bombing attack. (US Official)

Kinugawa Maru. The ship's foremast hangs limply over the port side where she has been driven ashore. Typically, when ships were attacked in anchorages surrounded by coral reefs or atolls, the ship's bow would ride high on the reef while the stern end sank in deep water.
(US Official)

action by Allied bombing compared to a loss ratio of about 85 percent for merchant shipping bears repeating. This point was noted by Chida and Davies in *The Japanese Shipping and Shipbuilding Industries*. It probably accounts for the timely way in which this key industry was able to turn over to a peacetime economy and respond to the country's need for national-flag ships to carry imported raw materials with which to refire Japan's other industries. It might also have been a matter of the shipyards being treated as secondary targets, with a lower priority than the munitions factories. Conveniently most of the major shipyards and virtually all the importation of raw materials were controlled by the same group of *Zaibatsu* described earlier in Chapter One.

Certain factors have been identified as critical points in the failure of the Japanese gamble to carve out an impregnable empire for itself in the Pacific and South Asia. These included the US Navy's victory at Midway when the Imperial Japanese Navy (IJN) lost its heavy lead in carriers and in effect never recovered its position of potential dominance. Although it quickly converted other ships (and lost them in subsequent engagements), once the American yards started to pour forth carriers from fleet size to escort, along with new naval aircraft which were equal to or better than Japanese models, the initiative was lost for the Japanese.

In retrospect, pouring assets into the Yamatos when so much else was deficient in research, new technology and up-to-date weapons was a disastrous policy. Radar, communications, bomb sights, escort ships, anti-submarine and mine disposal equipment were all outdated. A better designed and well-thought out emergency merchant ship replacement program, while evidently planned in part before the war, should have been ready for implementation after the attack on Pearl Harbor instead of two years later.

The Allies were at first in awe of Japanese naval aviation. With the redoubtable Zero fighter and some highly effective torpedo bombers, Japanese pilots pressed their attack with a ferocious determination capable of frightening anyone. In a matter of a year or so the famed quartet, the products of the American aviation industry—the Dauntless, Corsair, Hellcat, and Avenger—all started to appear and turned the tide against the Japanese.

The second major event was the retaking of Luzon, the main island in the Philippines which effectively created a huge salient, cutting into the relatively narrow neck that formed the northern entrance to the South China Sea, and included Hong Kong and the island of Formosa (now Taiwan). Here with American aircraft covering the entire sea, what had been a Japanese lake became one dominated by the Americans and nothing flying the flag of the Rising Sun was safe from quick destruction. The South China Sea was the key area on the main line from Japan to Singapore, the East Indies and Burma, and running the gauntlet became immensely costly. The South China Sea became a graveyard that claimed *Yamato's* sister *Musashi* and a considerable number of other Japanese warships, including some of its older battleships as well as a huge fleet of merchant ships.

The third major event was the advent of the atomic era whose A-bomb attacks on Hiroshima and Nagasaki shortened the war and averted more heavy casualties on both sides. We who were there in the Far Eastern theatre thought that Japanese resistance would be grim, although none I knew shrank from it. However, little did we know how bankrupt the entire state and military structure was of equipment and experienced fighting personnel, including pilots who had perished in great numbers flying kamikaze suicide planes. The Allies did not know, and nor did many Japanese it seems, the extent to which Japan was beholden to Germany for access to that country's research and scientific technology. Despite the difficulties communications were carried through by submarine over the entire distance after Germany's blockade runners and surface warships, which had been engaged in attacking commerce, had all been eliminated.

When Vice-Admiral Lord Louis Mountbatten's invasion force landed in Malaya in 1945 there was virtually no resistance. The Japanese heavy cruiser *Haguro* was the last large unit to be sunk by the RN in May 1945 and, so far as can be ascertained, no heavy unit of the Japanese Navy ventured west of Singapore after that date. When we arrived in Johore Strait behind Singapore we saw two more heavy cruisers beached and disabled each having had its stern and underwater section blown off or with heavy damage. These ships, *Myoko* and *Takao*, had originally been damaged elsewhere and taken by the Japanese to Singapore, presumably to be made ready for removal to Japan and major repairs. British midget submarines made certain that neither ever left Johore anchorage again and both were eventually dismantled for scrap where they lay or were removed and scuttled.

At no point did the invasion force meet up with any Japanese warship other than the above wrecks. We saw no planes, and it was as if everything had been spirited out of South East Asia and the Dutch East Indies area, leaving behind a rearguard of the Japanese Army and an array of the small 800- to 1,000-ton freighters, which by now were running the gauntlet through the South China Sea. Certainly there were many wrecked merchant ships in evidence and much bomb damage such as that in Singapore's dockland area; but there was not much in strategically unimportant areas. The highest priority had been to starve the Japanese of oil by destroying the East Indian oilfield installations, but it was interesting to note that the bunkering facilities at Pulau Bukam, Singapore, were apparently not touched as these would be needed immediately upon return of the Allies.

Our Royal Navy commando group landed amid the rubber plantations at Morib and again we were struck by the tidy way in which the Japanese had evacuated. We took possession of a small barracks just in from the foreshore at Morib. The Japanese Army had left it in spotless condition with a working cold shower, which our sailors greatly appreciated and used to wash off salt and sand.

The Japanese did not leave so much as a worn out bicycle tire or a notice on the notice board or even a thumbtack. We walked into the little town of Morib to find everything badly in need of some paint but otherwise clean and tidy. In a small creek we found a perfect example of a fishing vessel known as a *prah*. Her Malay owners had maintained her throughout the war in beautiful condition. She served the purpose of catching fish, which no doubt fed both the local Malay population as well as the Japanese garrison, as fish was a staple in the diet of both. While malnutrition was rampant in many parts of the Japanese empire, the bountiful land of rubber plantations also grew vegetables and fruit, grazed cattle and allowed the locals to keep a few pigs. With fish in plenty just offshore no one, natives or Japanese garrisons seemed to suffer any real shortage of food, other than of rice, a staple not grown in the area which had to be imported. The one critical shortage was tobacco which our return largely cured. For a few cigarettes local kids would shinny up a palm tree and throw down enough coconuts to give the entire group of us a treat.

To the north of us, Port Swettenham and Klang had been taken as had Port Dickson to the south, both in simultaneous landings. Beyond these the British forces worked their way north, east and south

An OSK liner from the late 1930s. Many fine ships were pressed into military or naval service. This vessel was a typical example. The following two photos show the vessel from both sides after she was driven ashore on a coral atoll. (OSK)

in a fan-like movement to entrap any remaining Japanese forces and sever their lines of communication. The northern thrust entered the important port of Penang to link up with another landing by a British group. Penang had been placed at the disposal of Japan's German allies as their Southeast Asian submarine base of operations in the Indian Ocean. When we arrived, Germany had already surrendered some months earlier, in May of 1945. It was here that U-boats restored and refuelled and set out for Germany carrying as much latex rubber and metal ingots as they could.

My first arrival at Singapore was a few weeks later. The city and its port remained interesting but very drab and run down. Commerce had restarted and the military held a tight reign on everything. The British were usually not the most popular colonial masters in peacetime, mostly because they were the most obvious and frequent, but the civilian population was overjoyed to have us back. We came with food, medical supplies and other essentials, plus an abundance of cigarettes. Money was starting to flow again and renewed purchasing power was evident everywhere. Women could indulge in their favourite cosmetics once again and everyone smoked cigarettes as if to make up for the wartime shortages. New Zealand and Australian produce was flowing into the shops and I tasted a superb New Zealand apple and sampled a prime leg of Canterbury lamb, items that I had not enjoyed since joining the Royal Navy a few years before.

Meanwhile, the process of rounding up the Japanese service personnel continued. A transit point and stockade was set up in the dockland area. The ubiquitous 800-ton Japanese Type E standard freighters could be heard from a considerable distance. They were powered by noisy Japanese-made diesels none of which seemed to be fitted with noise abatement mufflers. They came into the dock in steady succession each taking on about 500 military personnel who were shuttled to holding camps in the Dutch islands to the immediate south. Like us, the Japanese came in all shapes and sizes. Some were

A Type A freighter wreck at Hong Kong. A newly raised Japanese Type A wreck lies alongside a British navy salvage ship. The ship may be *Yamazawa Maru*, originally a Yamashita Kisen KK ship which was repaired and became the Chinese-flag, *Yenping*. The two Hong Kong yards were the only ones in the Orient outside Japan able to undertake heavy repairs in the early aftermath of the war and it is believed that repairs were effected there. (Heal Collection)

Chinese freighter *Yenping*. Following repair, *Yenping* became a unit in the Taiwan Navigation Company of Taipeh fleet. The strange looking oversize cowl mounted on the funnel is noteworthy, as are the original latticework derricks and the "see-through" crosstrees mounted on each mast. (R.J. Tompkins Collection)

tall intellectual looking individuals, others built like gorillas or junior sumo wrestlers, but most looked remarkably fit and all stripped to the waist, having had their uniform tops removed presumably to remove badges of rank so they could all be dealt with together, without protocols of rank.

Body lice and such diseases as ringworm could be a big problem throughout the East, but the Japanese, like the East Indians were very clean if given the chance. Presumably they were issued with fresh clothing at their next camp pending arrival of a larger ship to repatriate them to Japan, where, by the time they reached their homeland, it would be winter with snow in many places.

Japan was so short of large ships suitable for repatriation of its military from its former far-flung empire, that the MacArthur administration arranged to lend them a number of Liberty ships which had originally been outfitted as troop carriers. Two in particular which I remember were *Chief Joseph* and *Ancil F. Haynes*, both of which I saw at Hong Kong when they evidently called for bunkers and possibly to pick up Japanese repatriates in early 1946. As I recall, they were still painted all-grey except for a black funnel and sported the SCAJAP (Supreme Command Allied Forces, Japan) license number on the hull. They were flying the Chinese national flag, but their names had not changed at that point. If there were in fact Japanese repatriates on board there was no flagwaving, cheering or any other joyful expression as they returned to their badly destroyed homeland.

There being no further work for the RN Commando units, I found myself back aboard landing craft in Singapore in the immediate aftermath of the war. In the fall of 1945, our ship moved around to Johore dockyard for a repaint and some refitting as she was up for sale and would find a new home quite soon with a Sumatran rubber plantation company. A Japanese working party consisting of four men was brought down to the ship. We set them to work with chipping hammers and paint brushes and I have to say they worked hard and willingly and cleaned the brass ports as they had never been cleaned since the ship left the British builder's yard in 1942. The head man of the group, who might have been a corporal or equivalent, asked for some fine-grained graphite paper, which our engineer articifer found in the engine room, and it was this that they used on the brass ports and other fittings until they shone like gold. I think they cooked their own rice at lunchtime to which they added their own preferred condiments. We were not obliged to give them anything, but a little bit of humanity and generosity in the form of a few cigarettes paid a huge dividend in work willingly done.

On the second day we were joined on the other side of the dock by the m.v. *Arimasan Maru*, a modern pre-war Mitsui cargo liner which had been converted to a hospital ship. Given the state of most of the Japanese POWs we had seen we were surprised at the number of sick men loaded into the hospital ship. As there had been little if anything in the way of a shooting war in the retaking of Malaya, these must have mostly been casualties of disease or accidents probably concentrated at Singapore from a very wide area.

In view of the bestiality of the Japanese submarine arm, I had the satisfaction of being present as a spectator at the war crimes trials in Singapore, held in the best tradition of British military justice. I saw a variety of officers and NCOs sentenced to death or very long terms of hard labour. One of the worst was a general, at whose feet was laid much of the responsibility for mistreatment of Allied POWs on the "Railway of Death." This was the spindly Japanese military railroad built up the Isthmus of Kra and better-known from the movie *Bridge On the River Kwai*.

A school acquaintance, a British army lieutenant, worked on this railway and attested to it being every bit as bad, or worse, than portrayed in the movie. A Canadian friend, former Lieutenant Morton Mackay, suffered imprisonment at the infamous Changhi Jail in Singapore and barely survived with his life and sanity. Yet a third, Dave Murray was our accountant at a Vancouver insurance firm. Dave escaped ahead of the Japanese into the Malayan jungle and spent the war with a small band of countrymen making his way through jungles and across mountain ranges up to the Tenassarim coast of Burma. They eventually met up with an advancing British patrol. That survival trip engaged him and his mates for over three years by which time they were walking skeletons living on wild vegetables and fruits and off animals or birds they were able to snare. As he said later, anything was better than falling into the hands of the enemy. To the credit of the local population, themselves badly deprived, the fugitives were often given whatever help could be afforded in the way of clean water, food and periodic rest stops. Incidentally, most of the party made it in relatively good health with some of their weapons still intact.

When the war went against the Japanese they were no less resilient. Rather than surrender they holed up in the jungle to wait out the war and a return of their countrymen (who would not be returning as things turned out). Instances occurred after the war where individual members of some of the garrisons came out of the jungle ten, fifteen or more years after the end of the war. So fanatic were they, they would not believe the word of local people and the Japanese government had to send officials, including doctors, to pursuade them that the war was over and that it was now safe to come out. It was a moving experience to see one of them on Japanese television being returned to his wife and family after a very long absence.

Interestingly enough, while the many dramas of the Second World War were playing themselves out through 1945, such as the Allied retaking of Malaya, the recovery of Singapore and the two A-bomb attacks on Japan, another drama which has had very little attention was also playing itself out. This was the last voyage of German submarine *U234* which left Bergen, Norway, for Japan three weeks before the war in Europe terminated with the German surrender. Her commander, Kapitänleutnant Johann Heinrich Fehler, was carefully selected by the German High Command. The entire episode is set out in a carefully analysed account in the book, *Germany's Last Mission to Japan: The Failed Voyage of U234*, by Joseph Mark Scalia. This scholarly work opens up a whole new field of research to historians. Aside from describing the submarine, a Type XB minelayer, its crew and commanding officer, it also throws considerable light on this class of large submarine of a type sometimes used as a tanker or supply boat to the smaller operational submarines of the Type VII which were used mainly in European and Atlantic waters.

It is surprising to note that the war in Europe would be over by the time the voyage was into its third week, with many more weeks of travel ahead, as such a voyage was as lengthy as any that could be undertaken on the face of the earth without stopping anywhere for refuelling. She left Bergen, Norway, loaded to her maximum capacity with a great array of cargo. This included the latest Messerschmitt fighter, broken down into its essential parts, scientific and technically advanced cargo and drawings, plus a significant quantity of uranium oxide to permit Japanese atomic research. All this, according to Scalia's research, was in response to heavy pressure from Japan for more technical assistance from the Germans. The intensity of this pressure was probably as much a surprise to Japanese historians after the war as it was to the West.

When an armistice was announced all U-boats at sea received instructions from the Allies on how and where they should surrender. Boats were to be delivered intact, and mostly this was respected, although some were scuttled by their crews. Most of the crews recognised that their country was now at peace and to carry out further aggressive acts against the Allies would amount to piracy with all its consequences. Fehler was in a predicament. He had two Japanese officers as passengers for whom surrender was unacceptable. They were both of the samurai class and resolved the dilemma for Fehler when they committed suicide.

U234 surrendered to the US Navy on May 15, 1945. For the Americans it turned out to be an intelligence scoop like few others. The material on board alone was worth a fortune in the way of research, but just as valuable were the German military and civilian experts who accompanied the ship as passengers. Freed of the position as belligerents and with everything to be gained by co-operation, they spoke at length as they poured out state secrets of the Third Reich and provided many surprises for their American captors. This also illustrates the point made earlier, that Japan was in a state of deterioration. Its technical expertise, except for its prowess in shipbuilding and marine engineering, had largely fallen badly behind the Western powers so that, as the war came to a close in 1945, they were forced to beg for technical help from their German allies.

Royal Navy tank landing craft. An example of the small fleet of LCTs with which the author sailed from Singapore to Hong Kong, stopping on passage at the Brunei River in North Borneo to load pitprops for fuel-starved Hong Kong, where most of them were turned into charcoal. These ships were surprisingly seaworthy having sailed out from the UK under their own power, via the Mediterranean. The occasion was the vessel's launch from a British shipyard. (Royal Navy Official)

One incident that was first told to me by a young US Navy officer in Hong Kong concerned the loss of the *Awa Maru*, an NYK ship of similar size and design to OSK's *Arimasan Maru*, mentioned a little earlier in this chapter. An American submarine had torpedoed a Japanese freighter with very heavy loss of life in Formosa Strait, and apparently it had caused the American government and its navy a lot of embarrassment because the ship was sailing under a guarantee of safe passage as she had been on a mercy mission. The story and the ship's name faded from my memory until I engaged in research for this book, when I came across a recently released account of the whole incident in the book *Ghost of War*, by Roger Dingman. It was another of those extraordinary war stories which periodically show up following much patient research work on the part of an author who feels he is onto something especially significant.

The book clearly sets out the desperate state of affairs existing in the Far Eastern theatre of war. American and Allied POWs were in an appalling plight. Many had suffered the effects of brutality and a good many of these died as a result. The effects of malnutrition and disease were general through the entire POW population, and losses from these causes were known to be mounting and could only get worse as Japan's own predicament worsened. In fact, millions of her own people were only slightly better off as the effects of the onslaught on her shipping caused critical shortages of food and the relentless bombing of the main cities was laying waste to everything including the most basic necessities. It was of little concern to the Japanese government when the Hague and Geneva Conventions on the treatment of prisoners were cited as they could do little more, even for their own people.

When American and Allied governments expressed alarm on the treatment of their nationals, the United States entered into lengthy negotiations, via the Swiss and Spanish governments working through the Japanese legations in Berne and Madrid. Through this long drawn-out diplomatic exchange, an agreement was eventually reached by which relief supplies of medication, food and other necessities were to be shipped to Murmansk in the Arctic convoys and then transshipped by rail to Nakhodka about sixty miles away from Vladivostok. It was a long and tortuous journey. At that time the Soviets were non-combatants in the Far Eastern theatre. Under these arrangements a Japanese ship was to call at Nakhodka to load supplies and then, following a carefully laid-out timetable and itinerary, deliver the supplies to ports from which they could be delivered to the prison camps. The first two vessels selected, *Hakusan Maru*, and *Hosin Maru*, were smaller ships and evidently the arrangements went according to plan even if the Japanese were less than completely careful about the timetable.

The third ship selected for the mercy mission was *Awa Maru*, a vessel of prewar design which was under construction when Japan launched the Pacific War. She picked up her relief cargo and then made her way via several ports as far south as Singapore, where the final discharge was made including some cannon and other munitions which was contrary to the agreement made between the Americans and the Japanese. Here she loaded with rubber, tin and presumably any other strategic materials that could be organized for the return to Japan. She was also flooded with passengers, many of them of high rank, seeking a passage back to the homeland in the face of the crumbling Southeast Asian empire. By now it was the spring of 1945 and the war was within six months of ending. While the ship passed through Formosa Strait at high speed, with all lights blazing and in foggy weather, the US Navy submarine *Queenfish* shot four torpedoes into her at a range of 17,000 yards.

A salvaged freighter at Hong Kong. The vessel rides at anchor awaiting
removal. She appears to be one of the typical six hatch freighters which
Japanese shipyards built in numbers in the late 1930s. In a diving exercise
in Hong Kong harbour the author sat on the propeller boss of this ship and
contemplated the surrounding watery world. The shipyard in the
background is Hong Kong & Whampoa Dockyard, which was a unit of
the Jardine Mathieson group. (Heal Collection)

Awa Maru sank in a few short minutes taking over 2000 people with her. In terms of loss of life it was one of the largest single sinkings of the Pacific War although there had been worse in the European theatre. The submarine improperly identified the ship, thinking she was dealing with a destroyer given the ship's speed. It resulted in a court-martial for the submarine's captain and the incident was labelled America's biggest mistake of the war. It was an error which would have repercussions that would last for decades afterwards in American-Japanese relations.

The final anecdote in this chapter is an example of Japanese chivalry of a very high order. Sam Falle, author of the book *My Lucky Life: In War, Revolution, Peace and Diplomacy*, was a Royal Navy lieutenant when his destroyer HMS *Encounter* was sunk by gunfire from Japanese heavy cruisers following the Battle of the Java Sea. In this battle, units of the ABDA force, made up of American, British, Dutch and Australian warships organized as a loosely composed defence force under the command of Dutch Admiral Karol Doorman, fought a far more powerful Japanese force which was covering the invasion of Java.

Evidently the cruiser *Exeter*, Falle's ship *Encounter* and the USS *Pope* were the last survivors of the Allied force and were under orders to make their escape through Sunda Strait when all three ships sank under a hail of heavy gunfire. Falle, along with other survivors, was picked up by the Japanese destroyer *Ikazuchi* and treated with great humanity. With 400 survivors on board the destroyer was heavily laden, but the Japanese assisted everyone to clean up after their immersion in fuel oil, fed them, rigged latrines on deck and set up canvas awnings to provide shelter against frequent rain showers and the burning sun. So much was Falle impressed that he dedicated his book in part to Lieutenant-Commander Shunsaku Kudo, late captain of the Japanese destroyer, whom Falle considers saved his life.

An account of this event was published in *Proceedings*, the journal of the United States Naval Institute and it in turn brought an enquiry forty-five years after the Java Sea battle from former Sub-Lieutenant Shunzo Tagami, who had been the Japanese gunnery officer aboard *Ikazuchi*. He explained that Lieutenant-Commander Kudo had passed away and with the exchange of several letters, the former adversaries, Falle and Tagami became firm friends, which culminated in a visit by Tagami to Falle's home in Sweden where he lives in retirement with his Danish wife. Sir Sam Falle was knighted for his distinguished services to British postwar diplomacy which included British ambassador in Kuwait and Sweden. Shunzo Tagami owned a fish processing plant in the town of Wakkanaishi and became an adherent to the Anglican Church in Japan. Falle was a prisoner of war for the three years following his capture and confirms that, relatively speaking and by comparison with the experiences of others which were worse, his treatment was relatively good. He escaped the fate of some of his shipmates who were shipped to Japan aboard a Japanese merchant ship which was torpedoed en route by an American submarine with a heavy loss of life.

At the end of the war there was much speculation about the rivalry between Japan's army and navy. The army, which had originally been trained by the Germans, incorporated many of the Teutonic instincts for which the Prussians were often condemned, while the Imperial Navy had originally been

Arimasan Maru was a Mitsui Line ship built in 1937 and operated during the war as a hospital ship. The author's LCT lay close by while this ship evacuated wounded and sick Japanese military from Johore naval base. This ship was another of the typical six hatch vessels which were seen frequently on the West Coast after the return to peacetime service. (VMM)

trained by the British and had adopted many of the attitudes that the British were famous for, including a great ability to meet the enemy at sea and, if not to always win each battle, to eventually win the war. This was a philosophy which stood the Imperial Navy in good stead in the Russo-Japanese war of 1905. The RN's Nelson traditions were freely adopted by other nations, not least by Japan. The army was regarded as the face of totalitarian militarism in Japan while the Navy had a more relaxed reputation.

After the war, my first direct introduction to the Japanese, other than as prisoners of war at Singapore, was the occasion when the NYK liner *Hikawa Maru* made her first visit to Vancouver in 1952 to reopen the transpacific passenger service which she and her two sisters had operated before the war. The two sisters were the *Heian Maru* and *Hie Maru*, both lost during the war. A friend and myself were with a group from the Vancouver Board of Trade who were invited aboard for a traditional Japanese lunch in company with the Japanese consul, local officials and the ship's master and senior officers. The ship's personnel were formal but friendly and wanted to make a good impression. The usual welcoming speeches were made and then we were allowed the run of the ship which had obviously been restored at great expense for she was in first class condition. The passenger trade across the Pacific was in rapid decline however and after some minor promotion of the passenger service, I think the ship more or less functioned as a freighter until her withdrawal and preservation in Japan as a much beloved representative of a popular trio in particular and the NYK passenger liners generally.

PERSONAL REFLECTIONS

The material in this chapter, while it has little to do directly with the Japanese Type A, is meant to serve as general background to the state of affairs in the Far East and Southeast Asia, based as much as anything on personal, often eye-witness recollections.

It was in 1952 that I once again became fully aware of the Type A freighters in rebuilt form. For a few short years they were frequent visitors to Vancouver and West Coast ports and for me this completed the circle of my personal acquaintance with these interesting but much maligned ships. From the beginning of the 1950s they came in the interests of peace and commerce. As an insurance broker my contact with them was more or less continuous as they carried cargo for import and export clients. I have given a full description of them in the chapters that now follow.

Later in my career, I worked for an international insurance broker, Johnson & Higgins, Willis Faber Ltd., and came into contact with some of their Japanese trading company accounts, most notably Mitsubishi and C. Itoh & Company. Their marine insurance needs were underwritten by the Tokyo Fire & Marine Insurance Co. in which Mitsubishi held a controlling interest. It was probably an arrangement that survived the old *Zaibatsu* arrangements which were partially broken up after the war.

J&H did not have to fight for the business in the usual competitive way of the marine insurance market. Tokyo Fire & Marine probably settled on J&H because of its connections to the world's largest marine insurance market in London and the firm of Willis Faber, Alexander & Dumas Ltd., which was also the British connection of J&H. My duties occasionally took me into the trading company offices where I always found the personnel I had to deal with to be courteous in the extreme and welcoming in a modified traditional Japanese way. Later I looked after the local needs of Ishikawajima-Harima Heavy Industries, the shipyard group who also had an office in Vancouver for a few years. While the experiment did not last in their case, the relationship was as good as those previously described. They all adopted a simple Western given name such as Bill or Ken, as a working name for dealing with westerners. It was much simpler than trying to remember the sometimes difficult Japanese given names and was the Japanese way of getting around the more stiff and formal which had at one time been their way.

In the 1970s I undertook two trips to the Orient for another employer, the Bell-Irving group of Vancouver. While in Singapore I learned of a pressing need for a shallow draft, sea-going freighter which could journey a long way up Borneo and Sumatran rivers to load hardwood logs. No one had anything closer than paid-off LCTs available and their drawback was that they could not carry big enough payloads. What the market wanted was a vessel capable of loading high up the rivers but journeying to Japan if necessary, with a deadweight capacity of about 6,000 tons.

Bell-Irving had no interest in the possibility of a project but William Brown, a local Vancouver naval architect, and I came up with a design to fit the concept which we called the "Pacific Utility" ship. It had a deadweight of 7,000 tons, a maximum beam, shallow draft and twin screws with a bowthruster. Her cargo handling arrangements consisted of four single-acting booms mounted from twin masts which were placed at the extreme beam of the ship to maximize outreach. The ship had the capability of loading below deck while a deckload could be placed on heavy steel hatches in the usual way. Through a shipbroker, expressions of interest were solicited from a variety of shipyards locally, in Singapore, Japan and Europe. The Japanese response was impressive. Two yards came back immediately and one, Fukuoka Shipbuilding Company, sent plans over for a similar ship and made it clear that they wanted the business but did all those things that were calculated to impress us in a business-like way, and I'm sure that, had the project gone further we would have gone to Fukuoka. By way of contrast, most other yards outside of Japan, either ignored the request or came back with a half interested response.

Hull No. 1 at Mitsubishi-Hiroshima. During the summer of 1944, the new Type 2A ship *Hisakawa Maru* slides down the ways before a large audience. The person launching the ship appears to be a woman in white. Behind her are two military figures standing at attention. The shipyard was newly established which might have added to the excitement. Note the signal mast mounted on the starboard forward kingpost.
(Mitsubishi Archive)

CHAPTER FIVE

THE JAPANESE EMERGENCY SHIPBUILDING PROGRAM: THE STANDARD TYPE A AND ALLIED EQUIVALENTS

THE ALLIES HAD SUSTAINED SERIOUS SHIPPING LOSSES at sea during the war years and had instituted huge merchant and warship building programs in Canada, Britain and most particularly in the United States. So did Japan when faced with the same dilemma. The Allied Emergency Shipbuilding Programs not only centred on constructing some 7000 or more cargo ships and tankers—in the approximate 10,000 dwt classes and larger, plus many smaller vessels in the coastal or short sea classes—they also included a huge fleet of corvettes, frigates, destroyer escorts and larger naval vessels.

The lesson of the North Atlantic had shown that, no matter how many escorts were available to the Allies, they could often have done with more. This shortfall was only overcome when escort carriers entered the fray, closing the notorious North Atlantic "gap" or "black hole," the sea area that could not be covered by shore-based aircraft. Adequate air cover provided by carrier-borne fighter bombers, together with long distance flying boats and shore-based bombers adapted to sea service such as the Liberator and Lancaster types, enabled the Allied air forces to take on the U-boats. No doubt Japanese naval intelligence studied and evaluated the Allied experiences in commerce protection and anti-submarine warfare (ASW) arising from the First World War and through its listening post in Berlin kept itself well abreast of developments in the battle of the Atlantic throughout the Second World War. Even so, Japan built very few escorts during the war compared to the Allied output of escort vessels with real submarine-killing power.

Little was known about the Japanese navy's construction program for smaller vessels when the Pacific War started, and by the time Allied naval intelligence had been able to form any sort of a reliable picture, many smaller vessels of most types, not exclusively naval, had either been lost or had disappeared from the scene very soon after the war. *Jane's Fighting Ships* gave little attention to the Japanese navy's minor ships in its early postwar editions and such listings as they made were skimpy indeed. It is doubtful if *Jane's* ever achieved an accurate listing at this stage. There was no postwar use for these small ships and they were more valuable as scrap given Japan's circumstances upon the return to peace.

Evans and Peattie in their joint work *Kaigun: Strategy, Tactics and Technology in the Imperial Japanese Navy 1887-1941*, make specific mention of escorts with ASW capability under a subsection entitled "The Origins of Disaster." They pointed out that the Japanese Navy was indifferent to the problems of protecting the nation's shipping lanes and merchant shipping. All their thinking seems to have been projected toward two priorities. The first was the massive fleet action when the Japanese Navy would meet and overwhelm an opposing American fleet in one huge action, reminiscent of the first world war Battle of Jutland. They soon got their wish at the Battle of Midway when Japanese carriers took a terrible defeat in a battle that never saw conventional surface ships fire a shot against each other. It was a pivotal battle in the Pacific War. The second priority was to aggressively transport the army to its primary objectives in the island-hopping activities which pushed the Japanese empire to its greatest territorial limits. The navy's duty to deliver the army and its supplies was frequently criticized as an inadequate effort.

Several middle-rank Japanese naval officers were very aware of their country's deficiencies but, given the preoccupation of the Naval General Staff with such issues as future fleet actions, their views never received serious attention. The IJN did however, initiate a four-vessel building program for coastal defence ships of the Shimushu class which were to serve as general purpose escorts and carry out minelaying, minesweeping and ASW patrols. With so many functions packed into a small vessel it probably meant that these ships never developed their best potential in any one of them. The original projected tonnage was cut from 1,200 to 860 tons in an effort to save funds which then could be diverted to the building of the Yamato class battleships. A further fourteen more ships of the Etorofu class were ordered but none were completed due to stringent naval construction requirements when Japan went to war.

Hisakawa Maru. Her official completion date was September 10, 1944. This photo shows the ship on her trials, including the same paint patchwork at the bow as seen in the picture on page 78. *Hisakawa Maru* was an addition to the Kawasaki Kisen KK fleet, but her life was short. Four months after this picture was taken she was sunk off Taiwan. (Mitsubishi Archive)

GENERAL ARRANGEMENT OF THE CARGO SHIP Type 2 AT

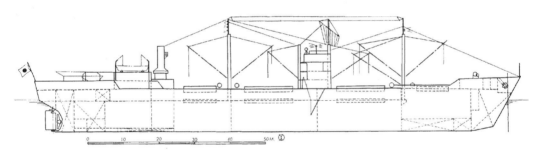

Type 2AT. Mitsubishi's trade book labels this side elevation view of *Hisakawa Maru* as a 2AT tanker, but whatever the differences were between the tanker and dry cargo versions, it is not possible to tell from this plan in the absence of tankage detail. It is thought that number 2, 3 and 4 lower holds contained tankage of a makeshift sort which was easily removed when the vessels reverted to dry cargo. So far as is known this happened with most of the survivors before the end of the war and none sailed as tankers in peacetime. Immediately after the war probably the bulk of the country's oil needs were brought in by American T2 tankers. (Mitsubishi Archive)

Most of Japan's available carriers, including those converted from large passenger liners, were lost in fleet actions. There is no confirmable record of smaller Japanese carriers providing air cover to merchant ship convoys, although several merchant ships and tankers were converted into small escort carriers of similar size to those developed by the Americans and British. Details of a standard Type 3TL tanker are given in Chapter Eight. This ship, *Yamasiro Maru* was commandeered by the army with the idea that they would also man and operate it, because they were dissatisfied with the IJN's effort in protecting army troop and supply ships. It was another example of the deep tensions that existed between these two branches of Japan's armed services.

Under attack. This dramatic shot shows two Type 2A freighters under aerial attack. One ship stands by while the other, with all cargo gear fully rigged, races away from the near misses of falling bombs. (US Official)

Top: *Encho Maru*. The first picture in this book known to have been taken immediately after the war, shows the first Japanese ship to reach Calcutta. Except for paintwork the ship is in original condition including the stovepipe funnel. (E.N. Hickling)

Bottom: *Encho Maru*. The same ship shows its utility boat davits and sheet metal ventilators which were probably made in bulk by small subcontractors in the way frequently adopted by all builders of standard ships. In the distance over the bow can be seen one of the British standard Empire Types. (E.N. Hickling)

When war broke out in the Pacific, Japan possessed, as noted earlier, one of the largest national merchant fleets, including a high percentage of modern tonnage but the Allied submarine campaign became so effective within the first year of the Pacific War, that shipping losses gradually strangled Japan's war effort. This in turn undermined its overseas garrisons and depleted the stream of war materials which were needed to sustain the Japanese forces. After Singapore there was primarily a token force of British submarines until about 1943 when the tide of war was turning and boats could be released from the Mediterranean. The Dutch Navy had submarines based at Sourabaya which put up a valiant fight against the Japanese invaders and then came under British operational control when they deployed to Australia, whence they acquitted themselves very well until the end of the war.

It was against this background that the Japanese government turned to mass production of standard classes of freighters as the demands of the wartime emergency intensified. The need for replacement ships became more urgent, but the pressing needs of the Japanese merchant marine were still subservient to the needs of the army and navy. There was always serious infighting between the two arms of the services, with the army dominating the politics of the nation, so it is perhaps not too surprising that a merchant shipbuilding replacement program did not seriously get under way until the war was almost two years old. By that time the merchant fleet had been greatly depleted and matters were becoming desperate. The merchant shipbuilding program was initiated and controlled by the IJN, who had, as earlier noted, started a program of design work as far back as 1937 in anticipation of an ultimate conflict. In this sense the navy fulfilled a role similar to that of the US Maritime Commission (USMC) and the British Ministry of War Transport. Its strength was that it could, at least in theory, more closely co-ordinate its naval activities with those of wartime merchant shipbuilding, but its weakness was probably the fact that merchant shipping was always secondary and subject to the dictates of the navy and depredations of the army. Both felt they understood the theory of merchant shipping needs but probably neither of them had much practical understanding of those needs.

One wonders to what extent the experience of merchant shipping management was utilized by the navy in its planning. Allied officers and personnel were encouraged to make their ideas or comments on operational matters known to their management. In some instances shipyards solicited, as a form of quality control, the comments of captains and chief engineers on matters affecting the operation of the ships in which they put to sea, particularly the warbuilt vessels. The reports of survivors following a vessel loss were all carefully collected and studied by the relevant authorities in the Allied countries and that was not confined only to the British or Americans. Smaller merchant navies such as the Norwegians also collected whatever data they could from their national flag vessels and personnel, and followed through with recommendations.

The Japanese mindset might have been different, as seems evident from the far higher level of casualties among seagoing merchant marine personnel. The lack of escorts, the absence of a recovery system—such as the Allies used in the North Atlantic with a designated rescue ship—and the Japanese attitude that life was expendable in the honoured service of the Emperor must have all added up to a terrible burden on crews.

THE SHIP CLASSES

Several classes of merchant ship were designed and built, covering a range of sizes from about 800 grt upwards, which are set out by class in the table below and detailed further in Chapter Eight. The Group 1 ships, those vessels in the first shipbuilding program of 1943, were generally take-offs from prewar designs. Thus, in the Type 1A shipbuilding program of nine vessels only three were built to the original prewar design, at which point the remaining six were converted to Type 2A, the design adopted for the 1944 program. All were of simplified design, lending themselves to fabrication on a large scale. The ships produced were a far cry from the good-looking, sophisticated designs of prewar years but given their purpose and the limitations of design and construction standards, they all served the needs of the nation as well as could be expected.

In order to utilize the traditional wooden shipbuilding resources which existed in Japan and in several of the conquered territories, a program to build wooden ships was also initiated. At the outset it provided for five vessel designs of 70 grt, 100 grt, 150 grt, 200 grt and 250 grt. Later the program was simplified to three types, those of 100 grt, 150 grt and 250 grt. All told 2,278 wooden vessels totalling 327,286 grt were built and NYK set up Yusen Kinkai Kisen KK to take on the mammoth task of operating the ships.

The warbuilt ships were in fact a far more radical departure from the usual Japanese designs, and can be contrasted to the position adopted by Britain, which had also been planning for wartime shipping as early as 1937. In the latter case the preference was for the adoption of designs already in successful production, being mostly the similar tramps turned out by East Coast yards with a long tradition of building practical, economical ships which were neither fast nor luxurious. These designs were the ancestors of the highly successful American Liberty ship. An example of British thinking was to be found in the "three 12s" design of tanker built in numbers for Shell, the British Tanker Company and Eagle Oil & Shipping. This was a very economical design for a 12,000-ton deadweight tanker operating at 12 knots and consuming 12 tons of fuel per day using Doxford diesel engines or similar that were built in the late 1930s.

This contrasted with the American position at the same time, wherein the USMC had concentrated on its successful series of three classes of Type C vessels, none of which really fitted the description of a trampship and all of which fitted American ideas of high speed cargo liners. The C1, C2 and C3 class vessels were all designed before the war, but during wartime they were to be joined by the C4 and the American Victory type (a distinctly different ship to the Canadian Victory type). In addition the USMC developed the T2 tanker of over 16,000 tons deadweight, or in excess of 140,000 barrels, at a speed of 15 knots. This highly effective design was closer to Japanese thinking on tankers that adopted designs which paralleled this specification during the 1930s, when Japan was securing much of its oil from the US. The T2 became the standard unit governing the oil charter market after the war in much the same way as the Liberty ship or its equivalent was the standard yardstick in the dry cargo market.

A useful comparison can be made between the T2 and the similar Japanese fast tankers of the 1930s. Until the commencement of the USMC shipbuilding program of the time, American tankers had not been noteworthy for superior features, particularly when compared to new European designs which started to leave the shipyards in the mid-thirties. Generally these European ships, while of superior design, were smaller than the Japanese tankers which would have been seen at California and Texas loading points. Could the Japanese ships have influenced American thinking in conceiving the design of the T2 tanker?

When America was preparing for a probable entry into the war she had little tramp shipping in a modern conventional sense. She possessed only the mostly obsolete remnants of a fleet left over from the country's efforts in the First World War, plus the new C classes of cargo liners. The Liberty ship was developed by the United States from the original North Sands design imported from Britain and, despite American contempt for old-fashioned, triple-expansion engines and a speed of no more than 11 knots, this vessel became the most-built design in maritime history. It was truly the workhorse of victory.

As with most leading shipbuilding nations, prewar Japanese designs and construction had reached a high art form fully comparable to that of any other nation and possibly more advanced than many. Certainly the ability to compete using high class passenger cargo liners in the service of major companies such as NYK and OSK was fully established. The result was that, when war did break out, the Japanese war machine had a high grade fleet of fast 16 to 20 knot cargo liners and tankers to draw upon, when the common standard for speed in the West was usually about 12 to 15 knots. Most of the best ships were quickly pressed into service as army transports or naval auxiliaries with some of the passenger liners being converted to light fleet aircraft carriers. This automatically added to all the reasons for potential shortages of merchant shipping from the first day of the war.

Chuan Maru. The former *Daiiku Maru* of OSK is shown in the colours of her second owner Chuoh Kisen KK who acquired her in 1957. She was deleted from the register in 1964 and presumed broken up at the anniversary of her 20-year survey as was typical with almost all of these vessels. (R.J. Tompkins Collection)

TABLE I
Description of the classes

The Japanese standard ship types were classified as follows. Measurements taken from Japanese sources are metric and could vary slightly within a class. Those quoted below relate to a typical sample vessel.

Class	Type	Length overall	Length betw perpendiculars	Breadth	Depth	Gross Registered tons (grt)	Deadweight tons (dwt)	Number built
1A	General/cargo		128.00	17.8	9.8	6400+	10425	(3)*
2A	G/cargo	137.33	129.91	18.2	11.10	6600	11200 (summer)	131
3A	G/cargo	137.33	129.91	18.2	11.10	7200	10230	6
1B	G/cargo		113.09m	15.8	9.1	4667	7336	16
2B	G/cargo							none built
3B	G/cargo		115.00	16.1	9.5	5100	7000	3
1C	G/cargo		93.83	13.70	7.6	2700	4476	34
1D	G/cargo		82.3	12.2	6.2	1900	2850	22
2D	G/cargo		85.00	13.40	7.2	2300	4000	103
3D	G/cargo		98.00	14.30	7.5	3000	4750	14
1E	G/cargo		60.00	9.5	5.0	830	1320	14
2E	G/cargo		60.44	9.5	5.45	873	1581	457
3E	G/cargo		60.44	9.5	5.45	884	1560	**
1F	G/cargo		50.00	8.4	4.2	490	771	21
1K	Ore/Cargo		120.63	16.4	10.0	5244	8433	20
1TL	Tanker, Large		153.00	20.0	11.5	9977	15600	23
2TL	Tanker, Large		148.00	20.4	12.0	9951	16600	33
3TL	Tanker, Large		150.78	20.4	12.0	9961	15067	5
2AT	Tanker, ex-cargo	137.33	129.91	18.2	11.1	6700		(34)***
3AT	Tanker, ex-cargo	137.33	128.26	18.21	11.1	7244		(2)****
1TM	Tanker, Medium		120.00	16.3	11.5	6400	10425	26
2TM	Tanker, Medium		93.00	13.8	7.3	2850	4722	43
2ET	Tanker, ex-cargo	same dimensions as 2E above						135
3ET	Tanker, ex-cargo	same dimensions as 3E above						none built
1TS	Tanker, Small		65.00	9.96	4.72	1020	1479	5

Notes

Yearly plan: 1943 - 1, 1944 - 2, 1945 - 3
*Six additional vessels converted to 2A design and included in next total   **no record of any built
***Included in count of 2A vessels above   ****Included in count of 3A vessels above

2AT and 3AT tankers converted from 2A and 3A dry cargo ships and included in their total. All survivors reverted to dry cargo after the war.

The foregoing are set out for comparison purposes. It is beyond the scope of this book to deal with classes other than the Type A on a ship-by-ship basis, although certain plans, descriptions and illustrations of the other classes are included. They came from Japanese sources and are set out in Chapter Eight.

Opposite top: *Daiitaku Maru*. Another of the NYK group, seen here looking smart in the colours of her later owner Daiko Shosen KK. She lasted until 1963. (R.J. Tompkins Collection)

Opposite middle: *Enshu Maru*. Possibly one of the first NYK arrivals at Vancouver prior to 1951. In that year she passed to Kyoritsu Kisen and became *Kyoan Maru* and then *Shin-ei Maru* of Kotani Kisen KK. (VMM)

Opposite bottom: *Eastern Trader*. In 1957 *Enshu Maru* passed to her final owner, E-Hsiang, a Hong Kong Chinese concern. In this picture she is seen getting underway in Madras Roads in 1964. Unlike most of her sisters she lasted over 23 years until her breakup in Taiwan in 1967. Fully laden and at this angle the Type A looks quite a handsome vessel. (Dave Edge)

The biggest dry cargo ship in the program was designated the Type A freighter, although at least two of the larger tankers of the Type 3TL were completed as other than tankers (see Chapter Eight). Built in three groups, Type 1A referring to the first program of 1943, only three were built to a design of clearly prewar vintage, with machinery amidships. The projected balance of that year's program of a further six vessels were converted in the contract stage to the Type 2A of the 1944 program. All had their machinery aft and 131 were built which made up the bulk of the fleet. Of the Type 3A of 1945 only six were built. The 1A certainly could have originated with 1937 planning when the Japanese turned their attention to potential wartime designs, but later the much modified 2A and 3A had little relationship to 1937 designs, except for dimensions. The evidence points to the 2A being put together in a near panic given the state of Japanese merchant shipping by 1943. The 3A probably embodied some improvements based on experience with the two previous groups of sister ships.

The dimensions of Type 2A are tabulated with others below. There was some slight variation in overall length between the product of one yard compared to another. With a grt of about 6,700 to 6,900 tons on average and an estimated deadweight of about 10,000 tons, assuming a more liberal wartime load line, these ships were roughly equivalent in dimensions to the common Allied Liberty ship size classes. Some of the Type A were fitted as tankers. In their case large tanks suitable for the carriage of heavy oils appear to have been fitted in the holds, even though they were not believed to be integral with the hull and could be easily removed to enable reversion to a dry cargo ship. It is estimated that the ships could carry up to 60,000 barrels. The conversion is believed to be similar to that undertaken in some Libertys and Canadian Parks.

The Australian Navy started its own standard River class. Like the British, American and Canadian classes listed, the Australian design was based on a British design, that of *Scottish Monarch*, built for the Glasgow firm of Raeburn & Verel Ltd, but only two were completed by the end of the war.

TABLE II
Comparative Table of British, American, Canadian and Australian standard types equivalent to the Japanese Type A ships.

Type	Length overall	Length betw perpendiculars	Breadth	Depth	grt	dwt	Number built
Japanese Type A	448.6	426.2	59.7	34.7	6,848	10,441	140
Empire A & B	446	431	56		7,036	10,202	520
Liberty	441.5	417.8	57.1	34.8	7,174	10,500	2,710
Ocean type	441.5	416	57		7,174	10,500	60
Park/Fort	441.5	416	57		7,130	10,000	353
Australian River Class	449.2		56.8		5.995	8.705	15

Note: Measurements in feet from Lloyd's Register for sample vessels in each class may vary a little from sisters in length and grt.

Most of the Allied ships shown above were powered with triple-expansion steam-reciprocating machinery, mostly coal-fired in the case of the British examples, but with a number of its vessels fitted with diesels. There were several British classes all of which closely approximated to the Empire A & B types noted above. The original North Sands design which was used in the Ocean and Fort/Park Canadian program was also a coal-fired ship. The Liberty, itself successfully adapted from the North Sands, and two later versions of the Fort/Park ships were oil-fired. The Australian ship was also coal-fired, but like many of the warbuilt ships, converted to oil after the war. Of all the Allied classes the one with the least variation in measurements was the American-built Liberty ship. In fact no variation has been noted in registers and this might have arisen because of the mass production, assembly line methods adopted by the Americans. British practice used far less in the way of detailed drawings, relying instead upon the experience of the skilled shipyard trades. The new American yards, lacking a large pool of highly skilled labour in the early 1940s, tended to utilize rigidly laid-out drawings for everything, which aided exact duplication. Japanese practice in terms of shipyard expertise probably tended to be closer to the British than the American.

Further detail on the several Allied types is covered in a variety of historical accounts which are listed in the bibliography. The British Type N ship from the First World War is dealt with in some detail below as it occupies a special place in this account.

As noted earlier, the original Japanese 1A design was a machinery amidships vessel with the necessary long propeller shaft and tunnel. Obviously, there was an eye to further economy in the 2A as it did away with the long shaft and tunnel of the 1A. In the 2A and 3A the engine room was located as far aft as possible, occupying the narrowing section aft to the stern gland. Ballast tanks and potable water tanks took up the balance of the space to the stern. As the ships would have been stern-heavy, compensating ballast tanks were located forward, with a big deep tank in lower No. 1 hold. A similar deep tank was built into the Liberty ship. This was missing in the Fort/Park class, and a common complaint was the difficulty in steering these vessels when in light condition with sea or wind on either bow, whereas more ballast forward would have helped.

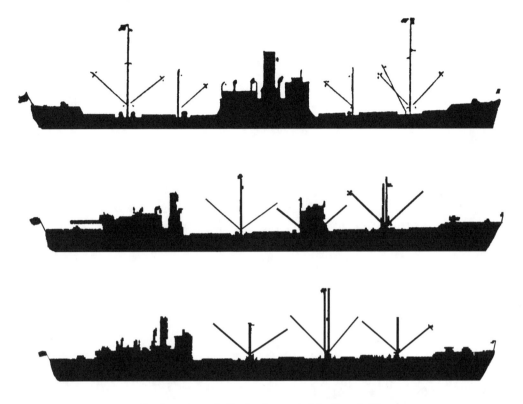

The three stages in the development of the Type A ship.

The hull of the 2A and 3A was so greatly modified from the original 1A lines as to have little relation to it. The stem was heavily raked with the forefoot coming to a sharp point with some uprise in the bottom, towards the forefoot, to make for an easy conjunction of bottom and side plating. There was neither concave or convex form in the bows, but the heavy stem rake allowed considerable flare as the shell plates were brought around to terminate at the stem. The butt ends of the shell plates were welded as was the practice in the Canadian-built ships with the longtitudinal overlaps riveted. The overlaps were usually tucked under a massive bowplate assembly, complete with hawse pipes in place. This assembly extended from the forecastle head down to below the loaded water line. The stem was tightly rounded sufficiently to obviate the usual stem plate to which shell plates were rivetted in older style construction.

Similar lines aft created unusual flare once the stern section was entered. They terminated at the stern in a very pronounced triangular "economy" stern, again without any concave or convex form in the shell plating. Generally it was a hull form not developed in peacetime conditions and, as with the British Type N, grew out of the extreme conditions which the British had to face in 1916-17 and which the Japanese anticipated in 1942-43 on account of the critical losses they were sustaining.

Except for the bridge structure in the 2A, it and the 3A ships had a long unbroken main deck relieved only by a short high forecastle, which when viewed from above made a nearly perfect triangle.

Opposite top: *Yamamura Maru*. Yamashita Kisen KK had one of the larger fleets of this vessel type. Here she is seen at Adelaide, S. Australia. Except for the funnel and an enhanced bridge and wheelhouse, she remained in original form. She was passed to Koun Kisen KK and only lasted until 1959, a shorter life than most of the other survivors. (Ian Farquhar Collection)

Opposite middle: *Eiho Maru*, shown leaving Brisbane in July 1958. NYK, with the biggest fleet of Type A ships, generally improved all its machinery aft vessels by replacing the stovepipe funnel with a well proportioned stack that did wonders for their appearance. (Warwick Foote)

Opposite bottom: *Etorofu Maru* seen at Mombasa. This ship had the distinction of being a part of the 1944 program, but was not completed until March 1948. No explanation of this long delay is available, but it is assumed that she was probably heavily damaged and could only be completed when the McArthur administration issued a long delayed license. (Ian Walker)

Approaching the stern there was a combination poop with internal living space and deckhouses above to form the aft accommodation. The decks had all straight crossbeams, thus eliminating deck camber. The bilges were constructed using standard formed quarter-round plate and were brought up to pinch out at the angular forefoot and stern. Although the act of forming might have been dispensed with as an economy measure, there was a great deal of heavy, plate-forming machinery spread throughout the Japanese shipbuilding industry so that it took little effort to preform plate and at the same time ensure a tighter and greater hull strength than would have ensued in a large vessel with hard chine bilges. The Type N by comparison had double chined bilges with internal angles of 135 degrees. As with the American warbuilt ships, both the Type N and the Type A and, so far as can be determined, all other Japanese emergency design ships, eliminated tumblehome, a more or less traditional design refinement which although it theoretically assists stability did not lend itself to wartime fabrication.

Every effort was made to economize on materials and methods to speed up the production process by using standardization throughout. There was no classification society supervision, and a number of innovations would never have been approved by such organizations (which provide the design and construction standards that guide most world shipping). One such innovation and probably the most critical, was the elimination of tank tops and, therefore, a double bottom in the cargo holds. This would have left the ships vulnerable to bottom damage with far greater consequences, virtually guaranteeing a total loss when a partial loss might have occurred to a regularly constructed ship in the same circumstances.

The midships bridge structure of the 2A was prefabricated ashore and then lifted as a complete unit with the bridge wings, external companionways and everything else in place—save possibly for the straightforward fitting of furnishings but even that could have been done before lifting the bridge structure into place. As this was done with the midships house, it was equally likely that the same was done aft, following installation of the propulsion machinery. Incidentally, that particular bridge structure and accommodation design—with its near perfect box form and a single-winged bridge at wheelhouse level, with cantilevered supports set at an angle underneath—started a design trend employed to this day in many bulk carriers and tankers. While economical and functional, the bridge wings were more exposed to extreme weather conditions when compared, for example, to the solid front, full breadth structure which had been popular earlier, particularly in Scandinavian ships.

When the few ships of the 3A design appeared, the bridge structure had been removed from amidships and taken aft where it was merged with the aft accommodation to form a single island, leaving all five hatches ahead to form an unbroken long maindeck to the forecastle. It was a precursor of the modern all-aft design which is now general throughout the world for modern bulkcarriers and tankers. It also increased the grt compared to the 2A but there was some loss of deadweight tonnage. It appears that at least two 3As followed the profile of the 2A with bridge structure amidships, but for further explanation see the notes in Chapter Seven.

The funnel in the 2A appears to have been the exhaust pipe protruding through the deck with a skirt of sheet metal around the base to deflect water. Beyond this, and without any discernible protective outer shell as with a conventional funnel, the exhaust pipe was evidently naked tubular steel, which must have been subject to constant corrosion from the effects of heat and airborne salt spray. The masts were a very light structure with minimal bracing and lattice cargo derricks. As soon as peace returned one of the first improvements made was to place an outer shell on the funnel. As ships were rebuilt, particularly those which were being brought up to cargo liner standards, the masts and most derricks were usually replaced by heavier masts and pole-type derricks. Another economy measure was to use light sheet metal for ventilators which were of a simplified design that could be turned out in any sheet metal shop. These were usually replaced after the war.

There were evidently so many complaints about the sparseness of the 2A that when the 3A came out there were some improvements in the specifications, among them an improved funnel, a necessity considering its now close proximity to the bridge.

Welding was used extensively but riveting was also used for many applications with the mix of the two probably varying from yard to yard. An account from Australia confirms that POWs were used considerably in the shipyards. A form of sabotage was to use undersize rivets in what became oversized holes so that once the rivet had been driven home and the leading end flattened it was difficult to discover. It affected the integrity of the structure because in a riveted ship a tight rivet becomes part of the strength of the vessel and a slack rivet undermines that strength. Slack rivets cause leakage and with enough of them, a reduction in structural integrity.

It is obvious that wartime emergency gave rise to the Type 2A design and others in the Japanese inventory of warbuilt shipping. What might be somewhat less obvious is what precedents existed for adoption of the design. Ships, shipbuilding techniques and ship designs are almost without exception an evolutionary development of a preceding shipbuilding technique or design which may have originated elsewhere. For example the Americans did not invent the all-welded ship; it was the British who designed

Opposite top: *Ehiko Maru*. Like some of her sisters, this vessel originally ordered by NYK was transferred to Kotani Kisen KK in 1945, probably just after the war. She is seen in Kotani colours, but was converted to a motor ship. She passed to Hong Kong Chinese owner E-Hsiang and was renamed *Eastern Carrier*. (R.J. Tompkins Collection)

Opposite bottom: *Ehiko Maru*. The "sawn-off" triangular stern which was a feature of these vessels was still something of a novelty. Comparison with the British Type N of the First World War shows that the Japanese, by increasing the flair at the stern and creating a near equal-sided triangle were able to gain much more internal space than in the N ship. (R.J. Tompkins Collection)

and built the first such vessels, a series of lighters used for cross-Channel work in 1916. This was followed by the first self-propelled all welded ship, *Fullagar*, constructed by Cammell-Laird, Birkenhead in 1918, initially as a shipyard prototype project which was acquired at completion by T & J Brocklebank, the well-known Liverpool shipowner. The Japanese might have led the way in the adoption of the bulbous forefoot first noticed as a prominent feature in their battleships of the Yamato class, but this is now standard in virtually all large ships. Something similar, but less radical was noted in contemporary battleships designed in the West in the late 1930s and during the Second World War.

As noted earlier, the author's theory is that a specific ship might have been the forerunner of the Japanese Type A freighter and some of the other designs. This vessel, *War Melody*, was the first Type N, fully fabricated, standard freighter to come out of the Harland & Wolff shipyard at Belfast. This design had been developed by Harland & Wolff at the instigation of the British government in order to speed up and augment the delivery of war emergency tonnage under construction at various yards including H&W. *War Melody* was completed as the war ended in November 1918, only to join the long list of ships the government wished to dispose of. Somewhat unusually for an American owner, she was purchased by the Robert Dollar interests of San Francisco and renamed *Grace Dollar*. Unusual, it is suggested, because there was by this time a great deal of new American construction available and coming onstream. Also, she was a coal-burner at a time when cheap California oil bunkers were fully available to West Coast owners. No doubt, Dollar switched her to oil as soon as possible.

In 1924, *Grace Dollar* was sold to the Japanese to become *Hakamatsu Maru* and she remained under their flag until lost during the war. Additionally, two other examples of the Type N ships passed to the Japanese flag when seized from Chinese owners in 1938, but certainly they had a great deal of opportunity to gain experience with *War Melody*. A comparison of her measurements with the Type A freighter *Enkei Maru* are set out below.

TABLE III

	British Type N War Melody (in feet)	Japanese Type A Enkei Maru (in feet)
Length overall	411.5	426.0
Breadth	55.8	59.7
Depth	34.4	34.7
Gross tonnage	6,500	6,848
Deadweight tons	9,400 est.	9,929 est.

The plan of a Type N shows that double-chine bilges were fitted and that they converged and pinched out just abaft the stem. As the bevel moved towards the stern it flared out to form the section of the hull which accommodated the tailshaft and ended at the stern frame and propeller. The side shell plating had a small flair at the bows with a straight-frame cross section from the stem back to the frame, forming the fore part of No. 1 hold. From then the frames were completely vertical without tumblehome until they reached just aft of the main mast when the longtitudinal curvature of the side shell plating started to turn in towards the centre line. At the point where it reached the stern it joined the stern triangular plate.

Unlike the Japanese Type A, some small regard was paid to aesthetics in the Type N. Some rising sheer was designed into the main deck from the foremast forward to the stem and from the main mast aft to the stern. In practical terms it was probably included as a design feature to help bouyancy and maintain a drier ship. It was just enough to avoid the ungainly, somewhat "hogged" look of its contemporary, the American Hog Island ships which were a fully prefabricated equivalent of the N ships.

A final point before leaving the N ships is that, while they were fully prefabricated and utilized riveting throughout, the builders still managed to bring large preassemblies together and join everything with rivets. Shipbuilders today, used to working solely with welding methods which lend themselves to prefabrication, would acknowledge this as being a considerable achievement.

A feature of the Japanese shipbuilding industry was the extent to which the Imperial Navy controlled its own yards and in wartime imposed severe controls over the non-naval yards. Britain and the United States both owned their own naval shipyards, but fell somewhat short of the scale enjoyed by the Japanese Navy. The percentage of total shipbuilding capacity of the naval yards is not known, but it was sizeable as these were generally the largest and most superior yards in the country. When the war ended all this naval shipbuilding capacity became redundant so that these yards were turned generally over to private industry. Kure Naval Shipyard, after being leased by Daniel K. Ludwig, as previously noted, was turned over to Ishikawajima Heavy Industries, while Nagasaki Naval Shipyard, which built the *Musashi*, went to Mitsubishi. Sasebo Naval Shipyard became Sasebo Heavy Industries and Maizuru Naval Shipyard became part of Mitsui Shipbuilding and Engineering Company. With world shipyards fully occupied with postwar work and with shipowners clamouring for early delivery the Japanese yards found themselves in a wonderful strategic position to offer early delivery of new ships. It was a timely opportunity for an economy still reeling from the effects of its defeat. By 1956 the Japanese were in a highly competitive first place among the world's shipbuilding nations.

New Georgia. The narrow form of the Type N stern can be seen on this Elder Dempster ship as she lies alongside Lamport & Holt's *Marconi* when both were in lay-up near Falmouth in the depression years of the 1930s. (Heal Collection)

Hashidate Maru. Several of the large warbuilt classes of tankers and at least one Type 2A were converted for emergency use in the whale industry, in order to feed the starving Japanese population who were badly deprived of essential proteins. In sending out whale catching expeditions, the McArthur administration saw the abundant Antarctic whales as a quick answer to a severe problem. Prewar whale products had been a standard part of the Japanese diet. *Hashidate Maru* was a former Type 2TL or 3TL tanker. Her wartime lines can be seen clearly enough disappearing into the ship's large stern structure with its slipway for hauling whales on board.

CHAPTER SIX

THE STANDARD
TYPE A BECOMES
A CARGO LINER

ONE OF THE ADVANTAGES FREQUENTLY AVAILABLE TO A WRITER in the West is the accessibility of public records in national archives, museums, libraries, ship enthusiast associations and private archives. The western mind, regardless of language hurdles, has a great propensity to record, analyse, criticize and extol the great range of historic records, books, material, plans, paintings and photographs that are stored away for posterity. To this can be added an enormous volume of anecdotal material that is available on most marine subjects, often through the popular and technical magazine press. The author's personal view is that while hard facts are what most marine enthusiasts acquire books for, it is the anecdotal material that fills in many of the blanks and adds colour and depth to an account. Anecdotal material comes from many sources and one of the best is often the individual who, when contacted by an author, permits his story or experiences to be incorporated into an account, often for the first time.

Unfortunately, for a book like this, dealing as it does with excerpts from Japanese merchant marine history, there is little available in the way of anecdotal material in the English language. Undoubtedly, there is an unknown quantity available to the Japanese, but with language as a frequent barrier little of

Opposite top: *Enkei Maru*. Some of the Type A ships bore no resemblance to their original configuration, as illustrated in the previous chapter. One feature that could be not be altered was the telltale lines of the hull. (VMM)

Opposite middle: *Enkei Maru*. These ships always looked best when seen from a quarter bow view, fully laden. Here *Enkei Maru* leaves Vancouver down to her marks, probably with grain. (VMM)

Opposite bottom: *Enkei Maru*. Typically downgraded from a cargo liner with NYK to tramp ship services, the same ship leaves an Australian port fully laden, now owned by an NYK associate company Toho Kaiun KK.
(R.J. Tompkins Collection)

this is accessible. Searching the ship enthusiast magazines, I have noticed very little on Japanese subjects, unless they are military or naval war stories which are usually told from the Allied point of view. New ships would occasionally appear in the technical journals as would stories involving the major shipping lines such as NYK and OSK. The trade press, such as the shipping journals, would also run articles on the subject of shipping economics, dealing with trends in Japanese shipping, and that was the general extent of available coverage.

Since the Second World War Japanese shipyards, with a greater eye towards export markets, have produced some very fine periodical books setting out general arrangement plans and photographs of ships built by the yards. Almost all of the photographs have been taken while on trials, when the ship was in new mint condition. These have great value in measuring progress, but beyond that, when going back many years, writers must sometimes resort to drawing conclusions after careful study of plans, photographs and available information to deduce what was in the mind of the designer or shipowner at the time of building. I drew a set of conclusions in that regard in mentioning what I earlier termed the Kawasaki standard ship, or "Stock boat". Likewise I theorized on the relationship of the Type A to the British Type N and in a less original way alluded to the history of development of the many almost traditional British designs which led to the several standard classes built in Britain, Canada and the United States during the Second World War.

As noted, an obvious problem is language and westerners' difficulty in understanding the Japanese script in use. As a result, very little anecdotal material finds its way into English translations. For these reasons anecdotal material is not readily available and I must draw on my own limited experiences.

One of the few books I have found in English translation was a very good one by Tameichi Hara, who was also an Imperial Navy captain. Hara distinguished himself in the Pacific War. His story included his experiences in command of the light cruiser *Yahagi*. This cruiser was leader of a destroyer escort group when the battleship *Yamato* went to her doom along with a substantial part of the escort force. This book, *Japanese Destroyer Captain*, gives an excellent impression of life aboard Japanese naval ships during the closing period of the Pacific War. It is also very critical of the leadership of the Japanese Navy and the wanton wastage involved in what amounted to the throwing away of major ships in something akin to kamikaze attacks. There seems little doubt that the opinions, battle and survival experience of those who were not senior commanders counted for very little. The same appears to have happened with experienced merchant marine personnel whose opinions counted for nothing.

When I arrived in India in 1944, the British were pressing the Japanese back in Burma. For India this was the primary front where the sub-continent's own security had been placed in jeopardy. The Indian press printed everything, in some detail, that was released by the censors on this particular war-front. This contrasted with the scant coverage accorded to the Burma front in the rest of the Western media. Except for Britain, which was heavily engaged there, the rest of the world hardly knew that a nasty, serious war was underway on this front, a fact borne out in many history books of the Second World War.

The Japanese Army had invaded a small area of Assam and Manipur, the tea-growing region in the extreme northeast of the country. Royal Air Force activity against the invaders was the first sign of a mounting counter campaign. One of the best accounts of this phase of the war in Southeast Asia is to be found in *Silently Into the Midst of Things*, by Atholl Sutherland Brown, a Canadian from Victoria, BC. He was attached to 177 RAF Squadron in Burma, flying Beaufighters against Japanese rail, land and sea communications.

Intelligence reports from 1943 onwards referred to the mounting losses of the Japanese Merchant Marine and how it appeared to be causing severe shortages of all types of imported materials in Japan, as well as slow strangulation of the supply links to her many island garrisons. Parallel to these reports were suppositions as to what was being done by the Japanese war effort to cover the loss of merchant ships. Sources of much of this intelligence came from Allied submarine commanders who found that, while targets among larger vessels were becoming more difficult to find there appeared to be no short-age of small freighters in the 1,000-ton range and smaller. These simply constructed vessels could be quickly built, but the strategy must have put a considerable strain on finding sufficient skilled person-nel, particularly officers, to man the vessels. The idea was that by providing a large array of small poten-tial targets, the losses when they did occur would be less harmful to the war effort. This was true to some extent and, even though it meant sacrificing the operating economics of larger vessels, there was to some degree safety in numbers. However, even that supposition was strained to the limit. Sutherland Brown's account confirms that he and his fellow aviators went after anything that moved and much else that did not. Similarly Kinsman's account of the activities of British submarines in Southeast Asia, referred to earlier, confirms seeking out targets which towards the end became almost non-existent.

The author first learned of a Japanese equivalent to the Liberty ship in a photograph, taken possi-bly through the periscope of an American submarine, that gained some degree of circulation in the West. It showed a distinctively different, machinery-aft freighter with masts and derricks which indicated it was not a tanker. It had the open-frame type of crosstrees on the masts that the Japanese had always favoured, that being a distinctive mark of Japanese design not usually adopted by other nations. It was not until reaching Labuan, North Borneo, in early 1946 that I came across a specimen of the type. I was then serving aboard HMLCT 913 on passage from Singapore with three sister ships for Hong Kong. We were following the slow steamer passage used in the typhoon season, skirting the easterly extremities of the South China Sea. This took us along the north coast of Borneo, past Palawan and up to a point opposite the Lingayan Gulf on the west side of the island of Luzon. Here our course took a sharp turn to the northwest away from the shelter of the Philippines, while we ran across the open neck of the China Sea for Hong Kong.

Eiroko Maru. This sister of all the NYK Type A ships
acquired a more handsome conversion than most of the
others with a very clean, uncluttered appearance, as shown
in this and the following photo. (VMM)

Opposite top: Like her sister above, *Eiroku Maru* was downgraded to Toho Line tramp ship service. After being employed on the North Pacific service she was used in the North Europe line when it was reestablished by NYK in the early 1950s. (R.J. Tompkins Collection)

Opposite bottom: *Yamadono Maru*. The Yamashita Kisen conversions of Type A ships gave them a tall, rakish look that was not quite as apparent in the ships of other companies. The difference was mostly in the thin tall funnels that Yamashita preferred. (VMM)

Below (top): *Yamazono Maru*. One letter in the name makes all the difference. This Yamashita sister ship is seen here leaving an Australian port. (Warwick Foote)

Below (bottom): *Yamazono Maru*. The same ship is shown arriving at Vancouver in her owner's transpacific service. Yamashita Kisen was established as long ago as 1904 and in the regrouping mergers of 1964 Yamashita took over Shinnihon. (VMM)

Diaretsu Maru. Following the various changes in the
Japanese shipping companies can sometimes be confusing.
This ship was first owned by OSK in their colours shown
here, but in 1949 she passed to Nihonkai Kisen who
probably left her on charter to OSK. Later she will
be seen in a series of photos in Daido Line colours.
(Ian Farquhar Collection)

Our escort, the frigate *Veryan Bay* instructed the four LCTs to lay at anchor overnight in a deserted bay on the southerly side of Labuan, facing the Gulf of Brunei. This was preparatory to loading cargoes of mining pitprops for use as firewood in fuel starved Hong Hong. We dropped anchor in the afternoon, some hundreds of metres away from a large wreck, about three of our ship's lengths in size. I took our shipboard dinghy and rowed over to the wreck, beaching the dinghy on the forward main deck of the ship behind the forecastle. She was firmly aground with only a little of the aft superstructure showing where the ship ended. Her back was broken aft of the midships house and it was fully evident that she had been badly burned out. The bridge structure was a mix of red rust with soot from the fire at almost every port. There was no identification of who she was, and it was not until many years later that I was able to confirm that she was in fact the *Eikyo Maru*, one of the thirty Type A freighters owned by the NYK line.

By the time I had walked around on the forward main deck and forecastle, the tide had fallen a little and it was dusk, a very short period in the tropics. As I rowed back to *913*, darkness fell and my crewmates were a little anxious for my safety, but I had our ship's riding lights to bring me home through the gathering sea mist which eventually became dense enough to blot out all visibility until the rising sun quickly burned it off the following day. We weighed anchor as soon as there was any visibility and as the fog dispersed, we made our way across the Gulf of Brunei to the mouth of the Brunei River to load our cargo.

Kinko Maru. Owned by Daiko Shosen, the ship is seen in OSK colours. Daiko was founded in 1933 and associated with OSK, merged with Baba Kisen in 1966 and became a part of the Mitsui-OSK group. (R.J. Tompkins Collection)

Daikai Maru No. 1. Built for OSK, she was transferred in 1952 to Tamai Shosen, who renamed her *Tatsutama Maru*. The Japanese shipping industry drew a distinction between owning and operating companies. Many of the smaller companies were owners, but not operators. They were primarily investors. While the larger groups owned ships on their own account, most combined charters with the operating divisions so that in some instances such big operators as Kawasaki and Sanko ran large fleets of vessels owned by others. Tamai became part of the Yamashita-Shinnihon group. (Ian Farquhar Collection)

Daizui Maru. OSK converted this ship around 1950 and then sold her to Sanko Kisen in 1956. Sanko, established in 1939, was a relatively small player until it took on huge chartering commitments in the 1960s, often using foreign owned ships ,many of which were built specifically to meet Sanko's requirements. The system worked favourably for Sanko until around the 1970s when oil price increases brought about a very sharp recession in world shipping industries. Sanko's predicament was so severe that it provoked a major crisis for many companies that had speculated on Sanko charters. (Ian Farquhar Collection)

Opposite top: *Seiko Maru*. This was the first large postwar ship acquired by Sanko. She was built in 1949 and was typical of the large number of dry cargo ships which poured out of the Japanese shipyards in the postwar boom. Sanko was not close to any of the large groups and kept itself clear of the major Japanese banks. To that extent it was unusual as being outside the *Zaibatsu*. When it experienced difficulties in the 1970s which led to its bankruptcy in the mid-80s, Sanko had grown from a small fleet, when *Seiko Maru* was delivered, into the world's largest shipping fleet, most of which was chartered tonnage. Sanko is still in business in much reduced form. (Ian Farquhar Collection)

Opposite bottom: *La Cordillera*. During the period from the early 1950s to the late 1970s, the Japanese economy was one of the wonders of the world. It led to some interesting charter arrangements of foreign ships. Buries Markes Ltd., the British subsidiary of French international trading company Louis Dreyfus et Cie, owned this ship, which visited Vancouver under Kawasaki charter. (Heal Collection)

My next close-up sighting of a Type A was at Hong Kong in 1946. One day a strange ship arrived at the Kowloon wharves. I recognized the distinctive island bridge structure as being the same as that of the Labuan wreck, with the typical see-through crosstrees on the two masts, following previously noted Japanese practice. It was evident that the visitor, the steamship *Yenping*, built in 1944 but newly acquired by the Taiwan Navigation Company Ltd. of Taipeh, was of Japanese origin. She had previously been *Yamazawa Maru*.

Taiwan Navigation, itself a recent incorporation in 1946 encouraged by the Kuomintang government, quickly became quite a large concern as elderly ex-American vessels dating from the First World War were added to prizes taken by the Nationalist Chinese. The details of the ship are set out in the fleet list, but typically they were found in a damaged or sunken state in a port that reverted to Chinese control following the Japanese surrender and was seized by the Chinese. The photo of *Yenping*, which I went aboard while she was alongside in Kowloon docks, shows a vessel with a peculiarly large cowl mounted on her funnel, rather like an oversize garbage can lid. In fact, it might have been a matter of removing the skirt or water deflector just above the base of the funnel when a new outer shell to the funnel was added, as there was a remarkable similarity in shape and size between the *Yenping* 's cowl and the skirt. This was presumably a product of well-known Chinese ingenuity in using up material most ship repairers would regard as scrap because certainly no such fitting was in place in the original as-built design. Both ships remained in the Taiwan Navigation fleet until after 1958. By that time most of the class had disappeared from the fleets of the main Japanese companies and had been transferred into Japanese tramp operators' fleets for a few more years of service.

It should be remembered that an embargo was placed on the building of new ships by the American administration following the signing of the armistice agreement in 1945. An exception was made with fishing and certain whaling vessels where either new construction or major conversion was allowed in significant numbers to maintain the supply of fish and whale products to the nation. This policy was pursued to redress the severe shortages in protein available to the population. Examples of ships converted, or completed, to revive the postwar whaling industry were *Hashidate Maru*, a former Type 2TL tanker, built in 1944, which sailed on its first whaling expedition to the Antarctic in 1946. *Tenyo Maru, ex-Hirato Maru*, was under construction as a Type 3TL tanker when the war ended, but was finished as a whale meat carrier. Another 3TL was extensively altered while in the construction stage and was launched in August 1946 as the whale-oil factory *Nisshin Maru No. 1*.

A fascinating and entertaining anecdotal account of the second voyage of *Hashidate Maru*, to the Antarctic whaling grounds in 1946-7, is given by David R. McCracken in his book, *Four Months on a Jap Whaler*. McCracken was an observer posted aboard ship by the MacArthur administration. The book was published in 1948, but was only recently found by the author.

Inevitably, some Type A ships were partly built at war's end, and only one 3A was delivered prior to the surrender. Two 2As and five 3As were completed many months later and even up to 1948. Details of these vessels, *Ishikarigawa Maru*, *Etorofu Maru* and *Dairetsu Maru No. 1*, are set out in Chapter Seven. No doubt an inventory of available shipping revealed many weaknesses, and some exceptions were made to the ban on new shipbuilding. Incomplete hulls like the above were finished off and war-damaged ships that could be salved were repaired and put back into commission.

An example of a salvaged ship was *Tonan Maru No. 3*, a whale- oil factory ship which had lain on the bottom at a Pacific anchorage for eight years following an aerial attack. She was raised, towed back to Japan, and in a period of six months completely rebuilt and recommissioned as a whale-oil factory. She was not a wartime standard ship but the illustrations give an indication of Japanese ability in dealing with this kind of work.

In 1952, I settled in Vancouver. By this time the surviving Type A ships had been completely rebuilt, or at least, in the case of those that retained the original configuration, brought up to ABS or Bureau Veritas standard. They were placed on ocean services of major lines to West Coast ports in Canada and the US as well as East Africa and Australia. NYK was able to reopen its Europe Line using *Eiryaku Maru*. In Vancouver, I was able to visit NYK's *Enkei Maru*, one of the rebuilds with machinery and accommodation amidships, powered by her original turbines. She was one of the thirty NYK Type A ships—like *Eikyo Maru*, the wreck at Labuan previously described—although in *Enkei Maru's* case she had originally been fitted out as a tanker, Type 2AT, in much the same way as some of the US Liberty and Canadian Park ships. The T was added to denote a tanker conversion, but any that survived the war quickly reverted to dry cargo and their original designation as Type 2A.

As originally built the majority of the ships had turbines while a few had triple-expansion reciprocating engines. A few were refitted with diesels by choice of the postwar owners. Details are uncertain as it was not until about 1949-50 that Lloyd's Register started to present an accurate description of the ships. The choice of fuel and machinery seems to have depended on what could be scratched together at the time of building. For that reason some appeared to have been coal burners and others relied on precious oil. So far as can be ascertained, any coal-burning survivors converted to oil as soon as practical on being returned to peacetime service. Those that were built and lost during the war never appeared in any Western register. Only such records as have been turned up since the war from Japanese sources give us any information and in some instances it is sketchy.

The designed speed was stated in Japanese publications to be 13 knots, which was in line with the Japanese preference for higher speed when compared to Western ideas, but their economical operating speed was probably closer to 10 knots. The ones that seem to have been selected for major rebuilding into cargo liners appear to have been those fitted with turbines. Those that retained their status as tramps incorporated minor improvements including peacetime funnels but retained their original wartime configuration. At least one example was extensively rebuilt as a bulkcarrier of a design common in the 1960s with all machinery and accommodation aft in a new modern-design superstructure, although cargo handling was the standard twin derrick arrangement to each hatch that was typical in that period.

For those ships that were extensively rebuilt to machinery-amidships configuration for postwar liner service, it appears that the American Bureau of Shipping was engaged to supervise the reconstruction to bring them up to a suitable class for liner service. As built, the ships had no double bottom except in the engine room. This was corrected by adding a new double bottom in the cargo holds. All the original housing and the lightly built masts and derricks originally fitted were removed or rebuilt and the machinery reinstalled in a new midships boiler and engine room. A new propeller shaft in a tunnel had to be built through what became No. 4 and 5 lower holds. A new long bridge deck was added from the foremast to the mainmast aft, leaving a small well deck at No. 1 and No. 5 hatches. The new bridge deck increased bale, cubic and deadweight capacity.

Monte Pagasarri. Spanish flag ships have always been a great rarity in the North Pacific trades. This 1959 Spanish built ship owned by Aznar of Bilbao was a Kawasaki charter in 1960 when she visited Vancouver to load grain for Japan, the only Spanish ship to visit in the author's 50 year recollection. (Heal Collection)

Opposite top: *Yamahiko Maru*. An early postwar new construction vessel for Yamashita Kisen, built in 1951. A turbine steamer, she could be regarded as the link to the wartime Type A ships, a logical development as Japan emerged from the shadow of its defeat in 1945. (Heal Collection)

Opposite bottom: *Kashii Maru*. This ship was built for Nittetsu Kisen KK, a smaller owner, and was operated in typical fashion by Kawasaki Line. The evolution from the Type A can be seen in comparing the hull of this new ship with a Type A photographed from the same angle. The new ship has a modest sheer and a more graceful, slightly concave stem, but with her long bridge deck and raised poop she looks remarkably similar to the standard rebuilt Type A illustrated in this book. (VMM)

The main accommodation had been aft in the original design but all accommodation was now shifted to the conventional midships position. Additional space was allocated for accommodation in the 'tween deck from the engine room, aft to the bulkhead between No. 4 and No.5 holds. In the split profile version of the rebuilt ship, No. 3 hold was placed between the bridge structure and the boiler room, with access in some instances through the boat deck. In other instances, No. 3 hatch was tiny and might have been dispensed with altogether.

An interesting matter for conjecture was how the holds were dealt with before the double bottom was installed after the war. The holds obviously contained internal bottom frames, but cleaning out a bulk cargo of coal without clear floors to sweep, for example, must have been a time consuming dirty job, most of it done by raw manual labour. Probably in practice the floors in the holds were lined with tropical hardwoods originating from Southeast Asia.

The lifeboat inventory was increased from two to four and new masts serviced heavier derricks sometimes supplemented by a heavy lift derrick probably up to 30 tons capacity at No. 2 hold. The "Ugly Duckling" appellation conferred by the author was less merited following reconstruction. In fact at certain angles and certainly when deeply laden, the rebuilt ships took on a sleekness that could not be said to be present in the original design.

I boarded *Enkei Maru* from a dockside gangway slung in place immediately forward of the bridge. The main deck had been lifted up at the foremast through to the mainmast to create the new long bridge deck beneath which was the new upper 'tween deck served through No. 2, 3 and 4 hatches. To avoid confusion, it should be remembered that the long bridge deck was not specifically related to the ship's navigating bridge and accommodation structure, all of which had now been re-erected along with the main accommodation in the conventional position for a machinery amidships vessel. The long bridge deck was integral with the hull and as noted this provided greater cubic capacity, useful in handling lighter liner type cargoes.

The main deck had evidently been coated with some sort of mastic compound that felt like sponge rubber when walked upon. This covering had been carried up the sides of the hatch coamings which gave the areas covered a distinctly well-worn appearance. The hatches were covered by hatchboards and the construction of the coamings was typical, but I never did find out the reason for the mastic coating on the decks in the vicinity of the hatches. Themasts were heavier than the originals and the derricks were probably new pole-type that replaced the original derricks, which had been of lattice construction. In addition new kingposts served No. 2, 3 and 5 hatches.

Individuality showed among the ships. What one owner saw as a necessity was not the view of another. This was particularly so with the arrangement of derricks although the configuration most used was that described above for *Enkei Maru*. The superstructure in this ship was new and had been fitted out to a good peacetime standard.

My host was the ship's second officer, a pleasant young man who introduced me to excellent Japanese Kirin beer. Unfortunately it was dark so any detail I examined was necessarily more difficult to see unless illuminated by the ship or shore lights. I did not see the engine room, but took a look at the bridge. Generally, the ship was well fitted out without a lot of frills. As noted earlier, she had been brought up to classification standards. My visit took place in 1952 and by 1955 *Enkei Maru* had been transferred to the Toho Line where she was downgraded to a tramp. Toho was an associate company of NYK which mainly functioned in the tramp trades. Her refitting was simply an interim measure because as new construction became available all Type A ships were transferred to other lesser owners and with very few exceptions, only lasted until the 1960s when they reached twenty years of age at most. At this point they went to the shipbreakers.

The Japanese standard ships were an interesting group for study by naval architects if only because they demonstrated how a very basic, unsophisticated steamer could be developed in an emergency and still function as a valuable and efficient postwar ship, until such time as newly constructed ships could take its place. It was exactly the same situation as occurred in Occidental countries with a pressing need to convert back from a war to a peacetime economy.

Western owners had many options as American, British or Canadian standard ships with a range of designs became available, from heavy lifts to refrigerated cargo liners to tramps. The Japanese had a more limited range with only the one basic dry cargo design to work with in this size and class. Considering just how basic the ship was they worked wonders. It was probably an exercise in originality rather than copying someone else's design and may well have been the forerunner of a new breed of Japanese naval architect and shipbuilder who quickly demonstrated their ability to meet international needs. Japanese shipbuilding before the Second World War was entirely taken up with building for its own flag owners or the Japanese Imperial Navy and because of the latter everything was generally very secretive. With the navy now reduced to a self-defence force and with the pressing need for exports the Japanese turned to foreign markets. By 1956, Japanese shipyards became world leaders in shipbuilding overtaking all Western countries in the process. They led the way in building ever larger and more technically efficient ships. If a foreign owner needed an extra 50,000 tons deadweight, the Japanese obliged and the international classification societies fell into line readily enough in developing and approving the technical specifications.

They had come a long way from the Meiji Restoration of some sixty years earlier. They had completed the *Yamato* and her sisters in the 1940s, and in a similar way they have come a long way to today, close to another sixty-odd years later, since they built the Ugly Ducklings of the Second World War.

CHAPTER SEVEN

THE TYPE A FLEET

Table I
ALPHABETICAL BUILDERS' FLEET LIST OF TYPE A FREIGHTERS

Note: KK refers to Kabusiki Kaisya, the equivalent of Limited or Incorporated Company.

Harima Zozensho KK.
Yards at Aioi and Matsunoura.

Amahi Maru
Daiha Maru No. 1
Daifu Maru (3TA)

Eikyo Maru
Kenjo Maru
Nissan Maru No. 1
Seiko Maru
Shiyo Maru

Tamon Maru No. 16
Tobata Maru (3TA)
Toshikawa Maru
Toyohi Maru
Yamazono Maru

Hitachi Zozen KK.
Yards at Innoshima, Sakurajima,
Mukashima, Chikko and
Kanugawa.

Yamaoka Maru
Yoneyama Maru

Ishikawajima Jukogyo KK.
Became Ishikawajima-Harima
Heavy Industries following merger
with Harima Shipbuilding and
Engineering Co. in 1960. Yards or
installations at Tokyo and
Yokohama; Chita added postwar
and Nagoya closed.

Daiai Maru
Daiei Maru
Daiga Maru
Daimei Maru
Daisetsu Maru No. 1 (3A)
Daitoku Maru
Eiroko Maru

Eitoku Maru
Enbun Maru
Esashi Maru
Hayahi Maru
Kenkoku Maru

Kawaminami Kogyo KK.
Originally Matsuo Zozensho.
Postwar became Showa Juko KK.
Yards at Nagasaki, Uranosaki,
Koyagishima and Fukahori.

Akikawa Maru
Daibu Maru
Daii Maru
Daijo Maru
Daikai Maru No. 1

Daikai Maru No. 2
Daiko Maru
Dairetsu Maru
Dairin Maru
Daito Maru
Daizui Maru
Edamitsu Maru
Eijyo Maru
Eikyu Maru

Eisho Maru
Encho Maru
Enpo Maru
Enshu Maru (Ensyu)
Eterofu Maru
Hoei Maru
Ishikarigawa Maru
Jakaruta Maru
Jintsugawa Maru

Dairetsu Maru. A selection of views which reveal the lines and details of a rebuilt Type A wearing the funnel colours of the Daido Line. This ship was actually registered in the ownership of Nihonkai Kisen KK, a typical Japanese tramp company whose mixed fleet of ships was employed mainly in the East. In the service of Daido this vessel ranged from the River Plate to the WCNA, East Africa and around the Cape of Good Hope. (VMM)

Jinyo Maru
Jokuja Maru (1A)
Kinko Maru
Kizan Maru
Meiyu Maru
Miyatama Maru
Nichiyu Maru No. 1

Nichiyu Maru No. 2
Ohtsusan Maru
Shingi Maru
Shirahi Maru
Surakaruta Maru
Taikyu Maru
Tatsuchiyo Maru

Yamaji Maru
Yamamiya Maru (1A)
Yamamura Maru
Yamateru Maru
Yamazawa Maru
Yamazumi Maru
Yuzan Maru No. 2

Mitsubishi Zozen KK.
Mitsubishi Shipbuilding &
Engineering Co., Tokyo. Originally
Nishi Nippon Jukogyo KK. Yards or
installations at Nagasaki, Kobe,
Yokohama, Wakamatsu,
Shimonoseki, Hiroshima and
Konan.

   Daietsu Maru
   Daiman Maru No. 1
   Dainan Maru
   Edogawa Maru

Eiji Maru
Eiman Maru
Einin Maru
Eiryaku Maru
Eiso Maru
Eiwa Maru
Ejiri Maru
Engen Maru
Enki Maru
Enoshima Maru
Enoura Maru
Erimo Maru

Esan Maru
Etajima Maru
Hisakawa Maru
Meishu Maru
Shinyo Maru
Shozan Maru
Tatsuhi Maru
Tonegawa Maru (3A)
Wayo Maru (3A)
Yamadono Maru
Yoko Maru (3A)

Mitsui Bussan Kaisha.
Originally Tama Zozensho KK. Yard
at Tamano. Tama opened postwar.

   Abukumagawa Maru
   Araosan Maru
   Arisan Maru
   Asakasan Maru
   Asokawa Maru
   Asukasan Maru
   Awakawa Maru (Awagawa)
   Azuchisan Maru
   Daibin Maru
   Daigyo Maru

Daihaku Maru
Daiiku Maru
Daiju Maru
Daisho Maru
Daishu Maru
Daitaku Maru No. 1
Ehiko Maru
Eiho Maru
Enkei Maru
Enryaku Maru
Kakogawa Maru
Katsukawa Maru
Kocho Maru

Kozan Maru No. 2
Meisei Maru
Mukahi Maru
Nakagawa Maru
Oesan Maru
Ojikasan Maru
Sagamigawa Maru
Tamon Maru No. 15
Tatsuhiro Maru
Tatsuyo Maru
Tenshinsan Maru
Yahiko Maru (Yashiko)

Nippon Kokan KK.
Originally The Asano Shipbuilding
Co. Inc. Also Tsurumi Shipyard.
Yards at Asano, Tsurumi and
Shimuzu.

Daishin Maru
Ebara Maru
Eikan Maru
Nichigyoku Maru

Shinyu Maru
Tatsuise Maru
Yamanami Maru

Table II
ALPHABETICAL LIST OF THE OWNERS

Note: Year of establishment, home port and the Type A ships are incorporated into the owners' fleets as first owners.

Alternative spellings of ship names are in brackets. War and marine total or major losses are noted in the individual ship list that follows. Subsequent changes of name and ownership are noted in ship list.

Baba Kisen KK, 1937, Tokyo	*Wayo Maru (3A)*	
Daido Kaiun KK, 1936, Kobe	*Amahi Maru* *Hayahi Maru* *Mukahi Maru*	*Shirahi Maru* *Toyohi Maru*
Dairen Kisen KK, 1913, Dairen, Manchuria	*Eisho Maru*	
Hachiuma Kisen KK, (Kensuke Hachiuma, Mgr, 1890) 1925, Nishinomiya Hyogo-ken (NYK Affiliate)	*Tamon Maru No.15* *Tamon Maru No.16*	
Hiroumi Kisen KK, 1887, Osaka	*Kocho Maru*	
Inui Kisen KK, 1934, Kobe	*Kenjo Maru*	*Kenkoku Maru*
Itaya Shosen KK, 1903, Otaru	*Yahiko Maru (Yashiko)*	*Yoneyama Maru*
Kawasaki Kisen KK, 1919, Kobe	*Akikawa Maru (Akigawa)* *Asokawa Maru* *Awakawa Maru (Awagawa)*	*Hisakawa Maru (Hisagawa)* *Katsukawa Maru (Katsugawa)* *Toshikawa Maru*
Kokoku Kisen KK, 1938, Kobe (Kawasaki Affiliate)	*Kizan Maru (Kisan)*	
Meiji Kaiun KK, 1911, Kobe	*Meisei Maru* *Meishu Maru*	*Meiyu Maru*
Mitsui Senpaku KK, 1895, Tokyo	*Araosan Maru* *Arisan Maru* *Asakasan Maru* *Asukasan Maru* *Azuchisan Maru*	*Oesan Maru* *Ohtsusan Maru* *Ojikasan Maru* *Tenshinsan Maru*

Miyachi (or Miyaji) Kisen KK, 1938, Kobe. (Related to Kokuku Kisen KK and Kawasaki)	*Shozan Maru (Shosan)*	
Naigai Kisen KK, 1922, Kobe. (Managed by Shinnihon Kisen KK)	*Tatsuhi Maru*	
Nanyo Kaiun KK, 1916, Tokyo. (Tokyo Senpaku Affiliate)	*Jakaruta Maru* *Jokuja Maru (1A)*	*Surakaruta Maru*
Nippon Yusen Kaisha (NYK), 1871, Tokyo	*Ebara Maru (Ehara)* *Edamitsu Maru* *Edogawa Maru* *Ehiko Maru (Eihiko)* *Eiho Maru* *Eiji Maru* *Eijyo Maru* *Eikan Maru* *Eikyo Maru* *Eikyu Maru* *Eiman Maru* *Einin Maru* *Eiroku Maru* *Eiryaku Maru* *Eiso Maru* *Eitoku Maru* *Eiwa Maru*	*Ejiri Maru* *Enbun Maru* *Encho Maru* *Engen Maru* *Enkei Maru* *Enki Maru* *Enoshima Maru* *Enoura Maru* *Enpo Maru (Enho)* *Enryaku Maru* *Enshu Maru (Ensyu)* *Erimo Maru* *Esan Maru* *Esashi Maru* *Etajima Maru* *Etorofu Maru* *Tobata Maru (3TA)*
Nissan Kisen KK, 1937, Tokyo	*Nichigyoku Maru* *Nichiyu Maru No. 1*	*Nichiyu Maru No. 2* *Nissan Maru No. 1*
Okada Shosen Kaisha, 1944, Tokyo	*Shingi Maru (Jingi)* *Shinyu Maru (Jinyu)*	

Opposite: *Meigyoku Maru.* Carrying a famous name on her hull, this ship's profile is shown off to good effect while at anchor in an Australian port. Nissan became a household name in the automotive world in the years after the 1960s when the parent Nissan Steel pushed its own line of Japanese cars. (R.J. Tompkins Collection)

Osaka Shosen KK (OSK), 1884, Osaka

Daibu Maru (1A)	*Daikai Maru No.2*
Daiai Maru	*Daiko Maru*
Daibin Maru	*Daiman Maru No.1*
Daiei Maru	*Daimei Maru*
Daietsu Maru	*Dainan Maru*
Daifu Maru (3TA)	*Dairetsu Maru*
Daiga Maru (Daiya)	*Dairin Maru*
Daigyo Maru	*Daisetsu Maru No.1 (3A)*
Daiha Maru No.1	*Daishin Maru*
Daihaku Maru	*Daisho Maru*
Daii Maru	*Daishu Maru*
Daiiku Maru	*Daitaku Maru No.1*
Daijo Maru	*Daito Maru*
Daiju Maru	*Daitoku Maru*
Daikai Maru No.1	*Daizui Maru*

Shinwa Kaiun KK, (date not known), Tokyo. (NYK Affiliate)

Hoei Maru

Taiyo Kaiun KK, 1917, Kobe

Taikyu Maru

Taiyo Kogyo Kisen KK, 1938, Tokyo

Yoko Maru (3A)

Tamai Shosen KK, 1932, Kobe (Toyo Kaiun Affiliate)	*Miyatama Maru*	
Tatsuuma Kisen KK (Tatuuma), 1910, Nishinimiya (out of busi- ness by 1952)	*Tatsuchiyo Maru* *Tatsuhiro Maru*	*Tatsuise Maru* *Tatsuyo Maru*
Toa Kaiun KK, 1939, Tokyo (see Tamai Shosen)	*Kinko Maru* *Seiko Maru*	
Toyo Kaiun KK, 1935, Tokyo (see Tamai Shosen)	*Abukumagawa Maru* *Ishikarigawa Maru* *Jinyo Maru* *Jintsugawa Maru* *Kakogawa Maru*	*Nakagawa Maru* *Sagamigawa Maru* *Shinyo Maru* *Shiyo Maru* *Tonegawa Maru (3A)*
Yamamoto Kisen KK, 1935, Osaka	*Kozan Maru No. 2 (Kosan)* *Yuzan Maru No. 2 (Yusan and Yuusan)*	
Yamashita Kisen KK, 1904, Kobe	*Yamadono Maru* *Yamaji Maru* *Yamamiya Maru (1A)* *Yamamura Maru* *Yamanami Maru*	*Yamaoka Maru* *Yamateru Maru* *Yamazawa Maru (Yamasawa)* *Yamazono Maru (Yamasono)* *Yamazumi Maru (Yamasumi)*

Opposite: *Wayo Maru*. A number of small Japanese companies invested in rebuilt Type 2A ships. This relatively good looking vessel, in Mitsui colours, was actually a Type 3A from the third year program. When this picture was taken in the early 1950s she was owned by Baba Kisen KK, the Tokyo based company, which owned only four vessels at the time. Baba was founded in 1937, as were a number of Japanese ship owning companies, at a time when capitalist interests were putting together small companies to own the many foreign built vessels with which Japanese owners, with government encouragement, were expanding their fleets. By 1966 Baba Kisen had become Baba Daiko KK, a merger of six small companies and a part of the Mitsui-OSK group. (Warwick Foote)

Wayo Maru. This was the only representative of the Type 3A to be completed before the war actually ended. Here she is seen riding light at Vancouver. Her original configuration is presumed to have been the same as shown for *Daisetsu Maru No. 1* at the end of this chapter. (VMM)

Table III
ALPHABETICAL LIST OF SHIPS BY YEARLY PROGRAM

Note: Ship fates given where established.

1A ships built in 1943 program.

2A ships built in 1944 program.

3A ships built in 1945 program.

Abbreviations:

ABS	American Bureau of Shipping	R	Three-cylinder steam reciprocating machinery
BV	Bureau Veritas		
GRT	Gross Registered Tonnage	T	Steam turbine machinery

1A CLASS VESSELS

Vessel Name	GRT	Completion date	Official number	Builder	Yard #	Machinery	First owner
Daibu Maru	6,441 grt	20.2.44	ON49926	Kawaminami	A2	R	OSK
4.5.44, Torpedoed and sunk by US submarine *Tinosa*, 250 miles SE of Hong Kong.							
Jokuja Maru	6,440 grt	8.3.44	ON50635	Kawaminami	A3	R	Nanyo
15.5.44, Torpedoed and sunk by US submarine *Aspro*, 250 miles NW of Caroline Islands.							
Yamamiya Maru	6,441 grt	31.10.43	ON49925	Kawaminami	A1	R	Yamashita
25.6.44, Torpedoed and sunk by US submarine *Bashaw*, off Celebes Island.							

The following were ordered as Type 1A, but plans were converted as 2A: *Dairin M, Eijyo M, Eikyu M, Jinyo M, Surakaruta M, Yamateru M*. Details listed below.

2A CLASS VESSELS

Vessel Name	GRT	Completion date	Official number	Builder	Yard #	Machinery	First owner
Abukumagawa Maru	6,887 grt	5.2.45	ON52651	Mitsui	395	T	Toyo Kaiun
1.6.45, Sunk by mine off Tokushima, Japan.							
Akikawa Maru (Akigawa)	6,859 grt	18.10.44	ON52781	Kawaminami	A35	R	Kawasaki
Completed as a tanker (2AT). 2.12.44, Torpedoed and sunk by US submarine *Sea Devil*, off the Shichito Islands, Japan.							
Amahi Maru	6,933 grt	20.4.44	ON51830	Harima	341	T	Daido
(See *Tenjitsu Maru* in end notes.) Completed as a tanker (2AT). 24.9.44, Bombed at Manila, Philippines. Believed a total loss.							

Vessel Name	GRT	Completion date	Official number	Builder	Yard #	Machinery	First owner
Araosan Maru	6,886 grt	30.4.44	ON50742	Mitsui	361	T	Mitsui

6.4.45, Torpedoed and sunk by US submarine *Hardhead*, in Gulf of Siam.

Arisan Maru	6,886 grt	22.6.44	ON50745	Mitsui	376	T	Mitsui

24.10.44, Torpedoed and sunk by US submarine *Snook*, 200 miles NW of Luzon, Philippines.

Asakasan Maru	6,923 grt	22.9.44	ON51748	Mitsui	386	T	Mitsui

Completed as a tanker(2AT). 18.11.44, Torpedoed and sunk by US submarine *Peto*, 100 miles SW of Korea.

Asokawa Maru	6,925 grt	14.9.44	ON51744	Mitsui	385	T	Kawasaki

Completed as a tanker (2AT). 28.3.45, Bombed and sunk by US aircraft, near Camranh Bay, French Indochina.

Asukasan Maru	6,886 grt	30.3.44	ON50732	Mitsui	358	T	Mitsui

4.7.44, Torpedoed and sunk by US submarine *Tang*, west of Mokpo, Korea.

Awakawa Maru (Awagawa)	6,880 grt	30.9.44	ON51751	Mitsui	387	T	Kawasaki

Completed as a tanker (2AT). 12.6.45, Converted to dry cargo. 10.8.45, Damaged by aircraft attack at Chongjin, Korea. No final disposition noted. Probably broken up at site.

Azuchisan Maru	6,888 grt	5.2.44	ON50407	Mitsui	352	T	Mitsui

2.10.44, Torpedoed and sunk by US submarine *Aspro*, west of Luzon, Philippines.

Daiai Maru	6,880 grt	22.1.45	ON52841	Ishikawajima	645	T	OSK

10.3.45, Torpedoed and sunk off Kamaishi, Japan.

Daibin Maru	6,886 grt	5.7.44	ON51737	Mitsui	377	T	OSK

4.10.44, Torpedoed and sunk by US submarine *Flasher*, off Iba, Philippines.

Daiei Maru	6,923 grt	18.10.44	ON52259	Ishikawajima	642	T	OSK

Completed as a tanker (2AT). 5.4.45, Converted to dry cargo. 3.6.45, Mined and sunk off Shimonoseki, Japan.

Daietsu Maru	6,890 grt	6.10.44	ON53399	Mitsubishi	685	T	OSK

Completed as a tanker (2AT). 31.1.45, Torpedoed by US submarine *Boarfish,* and then bombed and sunk by US aircraft off Quangngai, French Indochina.

Daiga Maru	6,903 grt	17.9.44	ON52258	Ishikawajima	641	T	OSK

1946, Seized by Chinese Nationalist government, allocated to Taiwan Navigation Co. Ltd., Taipeh. Renamed *Tai Peh*.

Shinyu Maru. This rebuilt Type 2A was owned by Okada Kaiun over her life of 18 years. Okada was related to shipbuilder Kawaminami Kogyo KK through Okada & Company, one of the smaller Japanese trading houses which would have ranked as a minor *Zaibatsu*. Seen here as a Showa Line charter, Okada Kaiun eventually disappeared into the Baba Daiko merger of 1966 and thus became part of Mitsui-OSK group. (VMM)

Vessel Name	GRT	Completion date	Official number	Builder	Yard #	Machinery	First owner
Daigyo Maru	6,892 grt	12.11.44	ON51762	Mitsui	390	T	OSK

Completed as a tanker (2AT). 7.2.45, Torpedoed by US submarine *Guavina*, 150 miles NE of Dungun, Malaya.

Daiha Maru No. 1	6,889 grt	19.1.45	ON54581	Harima	357	T	OSK

Completed as a tanker (2AT). 23.7.45, Mined and sunk off Karatsu, Japan.

Daihaku Maru	6,886 grt	28.4.44	ON50738	Mitsui	360	T	OSK

26.10.44, Torpedoed and sunk by US submarine *Drum*, 50 miles north of Luzon, Philippines. (Note loss of *Daisho Maru* below.)

Daii Maru	6,880 grt	23.8.45	ON50830	Kawaminami	A21	T	OSK

23.8.45, Mined and sunk off Yoshimi, near Shimonoseki, Japan.

Daiiku Maru (Daikyu, Daiikyu)	6,886 grt	10.6.44	ON51736	Mitsui	375	T	OSK

1957, Transferred to Chuoh Kisen KK, renamed *Chuan Maru*. 1964, Deleted from Lloyd's Register, broken up.

Daijo Maru	6,866 grt	30.3.44	ON50847	Kawaminami	A25	T	OSK

2.4.45, Torpedoed and sunk by US submarine *Sea Devil* 120 miles SW of Mokpo, North Korea.

Daiju Maru	6,880 grt	25.3.44	ON50726	Mitsui	357	T	OSK

23.4.44, Torpedoed and sunk off Shiono-misaki, Japan.

Daikai Maru No. 1	6,872 grt	27.2.45	ON54516	Kawaminami	A46	R	OSK

1952, Transferred to Tamai Shosen KK, renamed *Tatsutama Maru*. Converted and re-engined postwar to three-island type. Classed by ABS. 11.63, Broken up in Japan.

Daikai Maru No. 2	6,868 grt	26.5.45	ON54682	Kawaminami	A51	R	OSK

Converted postwar to three-island type. Classed by ABS. 1957, Transferred to Daiko Shosen KK, renamed *Daikai Maru*. 4.63, Broken up at Osaka, Japan.

Daiko Maru	6,880 grt	13.6.44	ON50856	Kawaminami	A23	R	OSK

10.8.45, Bombed and sunk by US aircraft at Rashin, Manchuria.

Opposite: *Taikyu Maru*. These two pictures illustrate the sharply functional lines and lack of all sheer in the hull of the Type A ship. *Taikyu Maru*, while outfitted as a cargo liner, called at Vancouver to load a full cargo of grain in the early 1950s. She was the only Type 2A in the fleet of Taiyo Kaiun KK who by 1952 had already taken delivery of three similar size ships of postwar design. (VMM)

Vessel Name	GRT	Completion date	Official number	Builder	Yard #	Machinery	First owner
Daiman Maru No. 1	6,888 grt	30.12.44	ON53642	Mitsubishi	689	T	OSK

24.1.45, Torpedoed and sunk by US submarine *Atule* in Yellow Sea.

Daimei Maru	6,923 grt	24.8.44	ON51966	Ishikawajima	620	T	OSK

Completed as a tanker (2AT). 3.11.44, Torpedoed and sunk by US submarine *Gurnard*, 200 miles Nw of Miri, North Borneo.

Dainan Maru	6,880 grt	3.12.44	ON53626	Mitsubishi	687	T	OSK

Completed as a tanker (2AT). 5.5.45, Bombed and sunk of Korojima, 25 miles east of Ikijima, Japan.

Dairetsu Maru	6,859 grt	20.10.44	ON52966	Kawaminami	A36	T	OSK

Completed as a tanker (2AT). 28.2.45, Converted to dry cargo, converted to three-island type. Classed by ABS. 1949, Transferred to Nihonkai Kisen KK. 3.63, Broken up at Hiroshima, Japan.

Dairin Maru	6,862 grt	27.2.44	ON50782	Kawaminami	A8	R	OSK

Laid down as Type 1A, completed as Type 2A. 3.7.44, Torpedoed and sunk by US submarine *Sturgeon*, 50 miles off Wonsan, Korea.

Daishin Maru	6,880 grt	30.4.44	ON51108	Nippon Kokan	472	T	OSK

19.5.45, In collision, sank north of Tsushima, Japan.

Daisho Maru	6,886 grt	30.3.44	ON50724	Mitsui	356	T	OSK

26.10.44, Torpedoed and sunk by US submarine *Drum*, 50 miles off Luzon, Philippines.
(Note loss of *Daihaku Maru* above.)

Daishu Maru	6,806 grt	28.8.44	ON51739	Mitsui	378	T	OSK

Completed as a tanker (2AT). 1945, Converted to dry cargo. 29.4.45, Torpedoed and sunk by US submarine *Cero*, off Kamaishi, Japan.

Daitaku Maru No. 1	6,888 grt	3.5.45	ON52662	Mitsui	399	T	OSK

Classed postwar by BV. Retained original profile. 1957, Transferred to Daiko Shosen KK, renamed *Daitaku Maru*. 12.63, Broken up in Japan.

Daito Maru	6,850 grt	26.9.44	ON50893	Kawaminami	A34	T	OSK

Completed as a tanker (2AT). 3.45, Converted to dry cargo. 9.8.45, Bombed and sunk by US aircraft off Rashin, Manchuria.

Opposite: Daido Line. The Daido Kaiun KK dated from 1936. As soon as commerce recommenced after the war it started a service from the Orient to the Pacific West Coast with their own *Mukahi Maru,* adding chartered tonnage as needed. *Dairetsu Maru,* illustrated elsewhere, was a chartered vessel as was *Kocho Maru,* owned by Hiroumi Kisen KK, shown here outward bound from Vancouver. (VMM)

Vessel Name	GRT	Completion date	Official number	Builder	Yard #	Machinery	First owner
Daitoku Maru	6,923 grt	18.6.44	ON51951	Ishikawajima	619	T	OSK

13.11.44, Bombed and sunk by US aircraft, Manila Bay, Philippines.

| *Daizui Maru* | 6,872 grt | 9.2.45 | ON53094 | Kawaminami | A43 | R | OSK |

Converted postwar to three-island type. Classed by ABS. 1956, Transferred to Sanko Kisen KK. 2.61, Broken up at Nagoya, Japan.

| *Ebara Maru* (Ehara) | 6,957 grt | 8.9.44 | ON51113 | Nippon Kokan | 473 | T | OSK |

Completed as a tanker (2AT). 25.10.44, Torpedoed and sunk by the US submarine *Tang* in Taiwan Strait.

| *Edamitsu Maru* | 6,873 grt | 6.2.45 | ON54464 | Kawaminami | A45 | T | NYK |

9.8.45, Bombed and sunk by US Aircraft at Najin, Korea. (See also *Enpo Maru* and *Erimo Maru*.)

| *Edogawa Maru* | 6,968 grt | 20.5.44 | ON51398 | Mitsubishi | 679 | T | OSK |

17.11.44, Torpedoed and sunk by US submarine *Sunfish*, in East China Sea.

| *Ehiko Maru* (Eihiko) | 6,888 grt | 30.3.45 | ON52658 | Mitsui | 398 | T | NYK |

1945, Transferred to Kotani Kisen KK. Classed postwar by BV. 1949, Converted to diesel propulsion and considerably rebuilt, with all accommodation aft. 1964 Acquired by E-Hsiang, Hong Kong, renamed *Eastern Carrier*. 19.3.66, Broken up in Japan.

| *Eiho Maru* | 6,888 grt | 5.10.45 | ON56643 | Mitsui | 401 | T | NYK |

Classed postwar by BV. Retained original profile. 1951, Transferred to Shofuku Kisen KK. 6.63, Broken up in Japan.

| *Eiji Maru* | 6,968 grt | 21.6.44 | ON51403 | Mitsubishi | 680 | T | NYK |

6.9.44, Mined and sunk 20 miles SE of Kaoshiung, Taiwan.

| *Eijyo Maru* | 6,863 grt | 23.12.43 | ON50639 | Kawaminami | A4 | R | NYK |

Laid down as a Type 1A, completed as Type 2A. 1.3.45, Aground, became total loss near Tsingtao, North China.

| *Eikan Maru* | 6,904 grt | 22.3.45 | ON51135 | Nippon Kokan | 477 | T | NYK |

26.6.45, Mined and sunk off Kamaishi, Japan.

| *Eikyo Maru* | 6,949 grt | 15.8.44 | ON51854 | Harima | 347 | T | NYK |

Completed as a tanker (2AT). 14.10.44, Torpedoed and damaged by US submarine *Dace*. Beached south side of Labuan Island, on Gulf of Brunei, bombed and burned out. Remains removed as scrap after the war.

Vessel Name	GRT	Completion date	Official number	Builder	Yard #	Machinery	First owner
Eikyu Maru	6,866 grt	26.1.44	ON50781	Kawaminami	A6	R	NYK

Laid down as Type 1A, completed as Type 2A. 21.9.44, Bombed and sunk at Manila, Philippines.

Eiman Maru	6,968 grt	2.7.44	ON52404	Mitsubishi	681	T	NYK

12.1.45, Bombed and sunk 25 miles NE of Binh Dinh, French Indochina.

Einin Maru	6,968 grt	19.8.44	ON52419	Mitsubishi	682	T	NYK

Completed as a tanker (2AT). 1945, Converted to dry cargo. Fitted as a refrigerator ship. Classed by BV. 1951, Transferred to Hayashikane Kaiun KK. 1953, Transferred to Taiyo Gyogyo KK. 1954, Converted to whale oil factory, all without change of name. 1969, Transferred to Daien Reizo as fish factory, renamed *Daien Maru*. 1976, Deleted from Nippon Register.

Eiroko Maru	6,923 grt	13.12.44	ON52271	Ishikawajima	644	T	NYK

Converted postwar to three-island type, re-engined and classed by ABS. Employed in NYK's postwar service to Europe. 1955, Transferred to Toho Kaiun KK. 1958, Transferred to Asahi Kaiun KK. 1963, Broken up at Onomichi, Japan.

Eiryaku Maru	6,890 grt	31.10.44	ON50953	Mitsubishi-Hiroshima 2		T	NYK

14.7.45, Bombed and sunk off Muroran. 26.6.47, Raised and repaired. Classed by ABS. 1948, Returned to NYK. 11.62, Broken up in Japan.

Eisho Maru	6,888 grt	31.10.44	ON52984	Kawaminami	A37	T	Dairen Kisen

Completed as a tanker (2AT). Dairen Kisen KK became Toho Kaiun KK. 2.3.45, Converted to dry cargo. Converted postwar to three-island type. Classed by ABS. 1962, Transferred to Shinwa Kaiun KK. 2.63, Broken up in Japan.

Eiso Maru	6,890 grt	11.12.44	ON53643	Mitsubishi	688	T	NYK

16.6.45, Torpedoed and sunk by US submarine off Muroran.

Eitoku Maru	6,923 grt	8.11.44	ON52270	Ishikawajima	643	T	NYK

Converted postwar to three-island type. Classed by ABS. 1955, Transferred to Toho Kaiun KK. 1962, Transferred to Shinwa Kaiun KK. 2.63, Broken up in Japan.

Eiwa Maru	6,968 grt	3.9.44	ON53396	Mitsubishi	683	T	NYK

Completed as a tanker (2AT). 13.11.44 Bombed and sunk off Manila, Philippines.

Ejiri Maru	6,968 grt	24.4.44	ON51397	Mitsubishi	678	T	NYK

10.10.44, Torpedoed and sunk by US submarine *Lapon* off Luzon, Philippines.

Vessel Name	GRT	Completion date	Official number	Builder	Yard #	Machinery	First owner
Enbun Maru	6,919 grt	25.6.45	ON52839	Ishikawajima	648	T	NYK

Classed postwar by BV. Retained original profile. 1950, Transferred to Yamamoto Kisen KK. 1959, Transferred to Tamai Shosen KK. 1961, Broken up in Japan.

Encho Maru		16.11.44	ON53091	Kawaminami	A38	T	NYK

Completed as a tanker (2AT). 4.4.45, Converted to dry cargo. Converted postwar to three-island type. Classed by BV. 1956, Transferred to Nissho Kisen KK, renamed *Nissho Maru*. 1961, Transferred Daiwa Kaiun KK. 5.63, Broken up at Onomichi, Japan.

Engen Maru		3.11.44	ON53598	Mitsubishi	686	T	NYK

Completed as a tanker (2AT). 6.2.45, Torpedoed and sunk by US submarine *Pampanito*, 260 miles south of Saigon, French Indochina.

Enkei Maru	6,892 grt	30.10.44	ON51757	Mitsui	389	T	NYK

Completed as a tanker (2AT). 12.45, Converted to dry cargo. 1952, Converted to three-island type. Classed by ABS. 1955, Transferred to Toho Kaiun KK. 1962, Transferred to Shinwa Kaiun KK. 10.63, Broken up in Japan.

Enki Maru (Engi)	6,968 grt	22.9.44	ON53397	Mitsubishi	684	T	NYK

Completed as a tanker (2AT). 31.1.45, Torpedoed and sunk by US submarine *Boarfish*, off An Nhon, French Indochina.

Enoshima Maru	6,933 grt	20.12.43	ON50610	Mitsubishi	675	R	NYK

22.1.46, While engaged in repatriation, mined and sunk off Chiang Kiang, near Shanghai. Of an estimated 4300 on board, 600 drowned.

Enoura Maru	6,968 grt	30.3.44	ON51390	Mitsubishi	677	T	NYK

9.1.45, Bombed and sunk at Kaoshiung, Taiwan.

Enpo Maru (Enho)	6,873 grt	11.1.45	ON53093	Kawaminami	A42	T	NYK

9.8.45, Bombed and sunk at Najin, Korea. (See also *Edamitsu Maru* and *Erimo Maru*.)

Enryaku Maru	6,925 grt	31.8.44	ON51745	Mitsui	384	T	NYK

Completed as a tanker (2AT). 1945, Converted to dry cargo. 17.9.45, Aground off Fushiki, Japan, in severe storm. Abandoned as a constructive total loss.

Enshu Maru (Ensyu)	6,872 grt	30.3.45	ON54552	Kawaminami	A50	T	NYK

Classed postwar by BV. Retained original profile. 1951, Transferred to Kyoritsu Kisen KK, renamed *Kyoan Maru*. 1957, Transferred to Kotani Kisen KK, renamed *Shinei Maru*. 1964, Transferred to E-Hsiang, Hong Kong, *Eastern Trader*. 8.67, Broken up at Kaoshiung, Taiwan.

Daikai Maru, fuelling Japan's postwar economy. Japan has drawn a great deal of its coal and other mineral imports from Australia and Canada. Here a fully converted Type 2A lies at an Australian mineral dock. Even though this ship had a better than average bridge and accommodation structure, it was impossible to hide the lines of the slab sided, sheerless hull as originally built. This ship saw service with OSK as *Daikai Maru No. 2* before passing to Daiko Shosen in 1957. (R.J. Tompkins Collection)

Vessel Name	GRT	Completion date	Official number	Builder	Yard #	Machinery	First owner
Erimo Maru	6,891 grt	20.5.45	ON53294	Mitsubishi-Hiroshima	6	T	NYK

9.8.45 Bombed and sunk at Najin, Korea. (See also *Edamitsu Maru* and *Enpo Maru*)

Esan Maru (Ezan)	6,891 grt	4.7.45	ON53305	Mitsubishi	7	T	NYK

Classed postwar by BV. Remained in original profile. 1951, Transferred to Hachiuma Kisen KK. 2.62, Broken up in Japan.

Esashi Maru	6,923 grt	7.5.44	ON51475	Ishikawajima	618	T	NYK

19.11.44 Bombed and sunk by USN aircraft, 14 miles NW of San Fernando, Luzon, Philippines.

Etajima Maru	6,933 grt	10.3.44	ON50616	Mitsubishi	676	R	NYK

13.9.44, Torpedoed and sunk by US submarine *Boarfish* in East China Sea.

Etorofu Maru	6,711 grt	31.3.48	ON54699	Kawaminami	A55	R	NYK

Converted postwar to three-island type. Classed by BV. 1955, Transferred to Taiyo Shosen KK. 1956, Transferred to Hokkaido Gyogyo KK. 4.62, Broken up at Nagasaki, Japan.

Hayahi Maru	6,919 grt	14.2.45	ON51367	Ishikawajima	646	T	Daido Kisen

13.7.45, Mined and sunk off Shimonoseki, Japan.

Hisakawa Maru (Hisagawa)	6,886 grt	10.9.44	ON50946	Mitsubishi-Hiroshima	1	T	Kawasaki

9.1.45, Bombed and sunk by US aircraft off Kaoshiung, Taiwan.

Hoei Maru (Houei)	6,859 grt	21.6.44	ON50890	Kawaminami	A29	R	Shinwa Kaiun

Converted postwar to three-island type. Classed by ABS. 1951, Transferred to Nittetsu Kisen. 1962, Reverted to Shinwa Kaiun. 12.63, Broken up at Tokuyama, Japan.

Ishikarigawa Maru	6,706 grt	25.12.47	ON54698	Kawaminami	A54	R	Toyo Kaiun

Converted postwar to three-island type. Classed by ABS. 1953, Transferred to Tamai Shosen, renamed *Tomotama Maru*. 1966, Broken up in Japan.

Jakaruta Maru	6,859	15.5.44	ON50857	Kawaminami	A27	R	Nanyo Kaiun

Completed as a tanker (2AT). 1945, Converted to dry cargo. Converted postwar to three-island type and re-engined. Classed by ABS. 1950, Transferred to Tokyo Senpaku. 2.62, Broken up in Japan.

Jintsugawa Maru	6,859 grt	10.6.44	ON50855	Kawaminami	A22	R	Toyo Kaiun

Class postwar by BV. Remained in original profile. 1.60, Broken up at Hiroshima, Japan.

Vessel Name	GRT	Completion date	Official number	Builder	Yard #	Machinery	First owner
Jinyo Maru	6,862 grt	27.12.43	ON50640	Kawaminami	A5	R	Toyo Kaiun

Laid down as a Type 1A and completed as a Type 2A. 6.4.44, Torpedoed and sunk by US submarine *Trepang*, off north coast of Luzon, Philippines.

Kakogawa Maru	6,886 grt	17.3.44	ON50720	Mitsui	354	R	Toyo Kaiun

13.11.44, Bombed and sunk by US aircraft in Manila Bay, Philippines.

Katsukawa Maru	6,886 grt	25.3.44	ON50721	Mitsui	355	T	Kawasaki

4.6.44, Torpedoed and sunk by US submarine *Shark*, 300 miles west of Ladrone Islands.

Kenjo Maru	6,933 grt	31.5.44	ON51851	Harima	346	T	Inui Kisen

Completed as a tanker (2AT). 7.12.44, Torpedoed and sunk by US submarines *Segundo* and *Razorback* north of Luzon.

Kenkoku Maru	6,807 grt	22.4.45	ON52855	Ishikawajima	647	T	Inui Kisen

Converted postwar to three-island type. Classed by ABS. 1951, Ashore at Point Reyes, 70 miles north of San Francisco, and refloated. 9.62, Broken up in Japan.

Kinko Maru	6,918 grt	18.6.45	ON54510	Kawaminami	A53	R	Toa Kaiun

1946, Transferred to Daiko Shosen KK. Converted postwar to three-island type. Classed by ABS. 1963, Broken up in Japan.

Kizan Maru (Kisan)	6,859 grt	27.5.44	ON50863	Kawaminami	A28	R	Kokoku Kisen

1954, Transferred to Sanoyasu Shoji KK, renamed *Izumi Maru*. 1957, Re-engined and rebuilt as a diesel bulk carrier. Bridge accommodation moved aft to a single-island structure. 1959, Transferred to Chuoh Kisen KK, renamed *Chusen Maru*. 1963, Transferred to Deh Ling Wu, Hong Kong renamed *Fastwind*. For at least part of this period under time charter to Kawasaki Kisen KK. 1970, Broken up at Hong Kong.

Kocho Maru	6,930 grt	18.3.45	ON52656	Mitsui	397	T	Hiroumi Shoji

Converted postwar to three-island type. Classed by ABS. 1961, Transferred to Daido Kaiun KK. 11.63, Broken up in Japan.

Kozan Maru No. 2	6,886 grt	29.12.44	ON52643	Mitsui	393	T	Yamamoto

6.5.45, Bombed and sunk, NW of Mokpo, North Korea.

Meisei Maru	6,886 grt	18.1.45	ON52648	Mitsui	394	T	Meiji Kaiun

1.6.45, Mined and sunk off Shimonoseki, Japan.

Vessel Name	GRT	Completion date	Official number	Builder	Yard #	Machinery	First owner
Meishu Maru	6,886 grt	14.11.44	ON53255	Mitsubishi-Hiroshima	3	T	Meiji Kaiun

15.8.45, Mined and sunk in Kanmon Strait, Japan.

| *Meiyu Maru* | 6,868 grt | 17.6.45 | ON54683 | Kawaminami | A52 | R | Meiji Kaiun |

Classed postwar by BV. Retained original profile. 1956, Transferred to Fuji Kisen, renamed *Taimei Maru*. 1959, Marine loss, probably collision, raised and scrapped.

| *Miyatama Maru* | 6,859 grt | 30.3.44 | ON50849 | Kawaminami | A26 | R | Tamai Shosen |

1.5.45, Bombed and sunk by US aircraft off Mokpo, North Korea.

| *Mukahi Maru* | 6,888 grt | 20.5.45 | ON56627 | Mitsui | 400 | T | Daido Kaiun |

Converted postwar to three-island type. Re-engined and classed by ABS. 1955, Transferred to Matsuoka Kisen, renamed *Shofuku Maru*. 4.64, Broken up at Mihara, Japan.

| *Nakagawa Maru* | 6,886 grt | 28.5.44 | ON50744 | Mitsui | 363 | T | Toyo Kaiun |

6.5.45, Bombed and sunk by US aircraft in the Korea Straits.

| *Nichigyoku Maru* | 6,903 grt | 25.5.45 | ON56334 | Nippon Kokan | 476 | T | Nissan Kisen |

Converted postwar to three-island type. Classed by ABS. 1960, Transferred to Nagoya Kisen, renamed *Meigyoku Maru*. 4.64, Broken up in Japan.

| *Nichiyu Maru No. 1* | 6,873 grt | 8.3.45 | ON54463 | Kawaminami | A47 | T | Nissan Kisen |

29.6.45, Mined and sunk off Shimonoseki, Japan.

| *Nichiyu Maru No. 2* | 6,859 grt | 30.6.44 | ON50780 | Kawaminami | A30 | R | Nissan Kisen |

21.1.45, Bombed and sunk by US aircraft off Kaoshiung, Taiwan.

| *Nissan Maru No. 1* | 6,889 grt | 15.3.45 | ON54577 | Harima | 358 | T | Nissan Kisen |

Completed as a tanker (2AT). 26.5.45, Mined and sunk off Shimonoseki, Japan.

| *Oesan Maru* | 6,892 grt | 28.11.44 | ON51763 | Mitsui | 391 | T | Mitsui |

Completed as a tanker (2AT). 11.45, Converted to dry cargo. Converted to three-island type. Classed by ABS. 1956, Transferred to Toyo Kaiun, renamed *Tamegawa Maru*. 1963, Broken up at Setoda, Japan.

| *Ohtsusan Maru* | 6,857 grt | 6.10.44 | ON52951 | Kawaminami | A33 | R | Mitsui |

Completed as a tanker (2AT). 12.1.45, Bombed and sunk by US aircraft, 25 miles NE of Binh Dinh, French Indochina.

Ishikarigawa Maru. Like *Eterofu Maru*, this ship appears to
have been one of the "afterthoughts" left over from the war
in either damaged or incomplete condition. They were both
listed as being a part of the 2A program from 1944, but
Ishikarigawa Maru did not appear until 1947. In any event
rebuilt as a cargo liner at some point she was renamed
Tomotama Maru for her original owners, Tamai Shosen KK.
(R.J. Tompkins Collection)

Vessel Name	GRT	Completion date	Official number	Builder	Yard #	Machinery	First owner
Ojikasan Maru	6,892 grt	15.10.44	ON51755	Mitsui	388	T	Mitsui

Completed as a tanker (2AT). 20.3.45, Converted to dry cargo. 13.6.45, Torpedoed and sunk by US submarine *Bonefish* off Inchon, Korea.

Vessel Name	GRT	Completion date	Official number	Builder	Yard #	Machinery	First owner
Sagamigawa Maru	6,880 grt	15.4.44	ON50737	Mitsui	359	T	Toyo Kaiun

7.5.45, Mined and sunk north of Karatsu, Japan.

Vessel Name	GRT	Completion date	Official number	Builder	Yard #	Machinery	First owner
Seiko Maru	6,890 grt	15.2.45	ON54611	Harima	356	T	Toa Kaiun

Completed as a tanker (2AT). 19.8.45, Mined and sunk near Nanao, Japan. 1.49, Raised and scrapped.

Vessel Name	GRT	Completion date	Official number	Builder	Yard #	Machinery	First owner
Shingi Maru (May show on some lists as Shinchiyo)	6,872 grt	29.11.44	ON54404	Kawaminami	A40	T	Okada Kaiun

Completed as a tanker (2AT). 6.5.45, Bombed and sunk in the Japanese Inland Sea by US aircraft.

Vessel Name	GRT	Completion date	Official number	Builder	Yard #	Machinery	First owner
Shinyo Maru	6,888 grt	6.2.45	ON55667	Mitsubishi-Kobe	690	T	Toyo Kaiun

8.1.45, Damaged by air attack 60 miles SW of Taipeh. Repaired. Converted postwar to three-island ship. Classed by ABS. 1963, Broken up in Japan.

Vessel Name	GRT	Completion date	Official number	Builder	Yard #	Machinery	First owner
Shinyu Maru	6,956 grt	23.10.44	ON53232	Nippon Kokan	474	T	Okada Kaiun

Completed as a tanker (2AT). 30.4.45, Converted to dry cargo. Converted postwar to three-island ship. Classed by ABS. 12.63, Broken up in Japan.

Vessel Name	GRT	Completion date	Official number	Builder	Yard #	Machinery	First owner
Shirahi Maru	6,872 grt	28.3.45	ON54551	Kawaminami	A49	T	Daido Kauin

13.6.45, Mined and sunk near Shimonoseki, Japan.

Vessel Name	GRT	Completion date	Official number	Builder	Yard #	Machinery	First owner
Shiyo Maru	6,933 grt	15.3.44	ON51828	Harima	319	T	Toyo Kaiun

Completed as a tanker (2AT). 23.11.44, Torpedoed and sunk by US submarine *Picuda*, off the west coast of Tsushima.

Vessel Name	GRT	Completion date	Official number	Builder	Yard #	Machinery	First owner
Shozan Maru	6,890 grt	20.2.45	ON53260	Mitsubishi-Hiroshima	4	T	Miyachi Kisen

26.5.45, Mined and sunk near Ube, Japan. Raised and put back in postwar service. Converted to three-island ship. Classed by ABS. 1964, Transferred to Sigma Shipping Co. (Trinity Development Co.) Hong Kong, renamed *Oriental*. 24.9.64, Caught in typhoon off Kimanoto Kasedashi, Japan, on passage Dairen to Chiba, cargo of pig iron. Broke in two. Sold for scrap.

Vessel Name	GRT	Completion date	Official number	Builder	Yard #	Machinery	First owner
Surakaruta Maru	6,886 grt	24.3.44	ON50831	Kawaminami	A9	R	Nanyo Kaiun

Laid down as Type 1A, completed as 2A. 21.9.44, Bombed and sunk by US aircraft off west coast of Luzon, Philippines.

Vessel Name	GRT	Completion date	Official number	Builder	Yard #	Machinery	First owner
Taikyu Maru	6,872 grt	5.1.45	ON53092	Kawaminami	A41	R	Taiyo Kaiun

Converted to three-island ship. Classed by ABS. 1960, Transferred to Hashimoto Kisen KK. 1964, Broken up in Japan.

Tamon Maru No. 15	6,925 grt	5.9.44	ON51743	Mitsui	379	T	Hachiuma Kisen

Completed as a tanker (2AT). 26.1.45, Mined and sunk off Hone Cape, French Indochina.

Tamon Maru No. l6	6,886 grt	30.11.44	ON52335	Harima	349	T	Hachiuma Kisen

Completed as a tanker (2AT). 12.8.45, Mined and sunk 100 miles NW of Iki Rettoshima, Japan. Salvaged and put back into service as a dry cargo ship in the early postwar. Converted postwar to three-island ship. Classed by BV. 8.63, Broken up at Onomichi, Japan.

Tatsuchiyo Maru	6,873 grt	20.3.45	ON54517	Kawaminami	A48	T	Tatsuuma Kisen

6.5.45, Bombed and sunk by US aircraft, SW of Mokpo, North Korea.

Tatsuhi Maru	6,890 grt	30.3.45	ON53273	Mitsubishi	5	T	Naigai Kisen

Converted postwar to three-island ship. Classed by ABS. 1964, Broken up in Japan.

Tatsuhiro Maru	6,886 grt	18.5.44	ON50743	Mitsubishi	362	T	Tatsuuma Kisen

5.10.44, Torpedoed by US submarine *Cod* in Mindoro Strait, Philippines.

Tatsuise Maru	6,902 grt	28.12.45	ON56337	Nippon Kokan	478	T	Tatsuuma Kisen

1952, Deleted from register. Fate not ascertained, but probably in damaged condition and not worth repair.

Tatsuyo Maru	6,440 grt	7.12.44	ON52638	Mitsui	392	T	Tatsuuma Kisen

Completed as a tanker (2AT). 8.1.45, Torpedoed and sunk by US submarine *Barb*, 30 miles NW of Taichung, Taiwan.

Tenshinsan Maru	6,886 grt	15.2.44	ON50716	Mitsui	353	T	Mitsui

6.5.44, Torpedoed and sunk by US submarine *Gurnard*, 50 miles NW of Menado, Philippines. (See note page 150.)

Toshikawa Maru	6,440 grt	15.3.44	ON55105	Harima	318	T	Kawasaki KK

Completed as a tanker (2AT). 19.10.44, Bombed and sunk by aircraft off Manila, Philippines.

Vessel Name	GRT	Completion date	Official number	Builder	Yard #	Machinery	First owner
Toyohi Maru	6,436 grt	30.12.44	ON51078	Harima	316	T	Daido Kaiun

Completed as a tanker (2AT). 4.5.44, Torpedoed and sunk by US submarine *Tinosa*, 250 miles SE of Hong Kong.

Vessel Name	GRT	Completion date	Official number	Builder	Yard #	Machinery	First owner
Yahiko Maru	6,888 grt	24.2.45	ON52655	Mitsui	396	T	Itaya Kisen

Completed as a tanker (2AT). Converted to three-island type. Classed by BV.7.1.62, Broken up in Japan.

Vessel Name	GRT	Completion date	Official number	Builder	Yard #	Machinery	First owner
Yamadono Maru	6,888 grt	5.3.45	ON55666	Mitsubishi-Kobe	691	T	Yamashita Kisen

Converted postwar to three-island type. Classed by ABS. 1956, Transferred to Nakamura Kisen KK, renamed *Asaharu Maru*. 1964, Broken up in Japan.

Vessel Name	GRT	Completion date	Official number	Builder	Yard #	Machinery	First owner
Yamaji Maru	6,440 grt	20.2.45	ON54405	Kawaminami	A44	R	Yamashita Kisen

2.7.45, Mined and sunk near Tokushima, Japan.

Vessel Name	GRT	Completion date	Official number	Builder	Yard #	Machinery	First owner
Yamamura Maru	6,859 grt	20.9.44	ON50892	Kawaminami	A32	R	Yamashita Kisen

Completed as a tanker (2AT). 15.3.45, Converted to dry cargo. 1956, Transferred to Koun Kisen KK. 9.59, Broken up at Osaka, Japan.

Vessel Name	GRT	Completion date	Official number	Builder	Yard #	Machinery	First owner
Yamanami Maru	6,945 grt	15.1.45	ON54626	Nippon Kokan	475	T	Yamashita Kisen

Completed as a tanker (2AT). 10.3.45, Converted to dry cargo. 27.8.45, Mined and sunk at Nanao, Japan.

Vessel Name	GRT	Completion date	Official number	Builder	Yard #	Machinery	First owner
Yamaoka Maru	6,932 grt	10.6.45	ON50491	Hitachi	not available	T	Yamashita Kisen

4.7.45, Torpedoed and sunk by US submarine *Tang*, 100 miles north of Mokpo, North Korea.

Vessel Name	GRT	Completion date	Official number	Builder	Yard #	Machinery	First owner
Yamateru Maru	6,862 grt	23.2.44	ON50803	Kawaminami	A7	R	Yamashita Kisen

Laid down as a Type 1A, but completed as a 2A. 24.8.44, Torpedoed and sunk by US submarine *Croaker*, 50 miles NW of Mokpo, North Korea.

Vessel Name	GRT	Completion date	Official number	Builder	Yard #	Machinery	First owner
Yamazawa Maru	6,889 grt	6.12.44	ON54403	Kawaminami	A39	T	Yamashita Kisen

Completed as a tanker (2AT). 21.1.45, Bombed and sunk off Kaoshiung, Taiwan. 1946, Raised, repaired and place in service as *Yenping* of Taiwan Navigation Company, Taipeh. 1968, Broken up in Taiwan.

One of the few sales to foreigners. The first picture shows *Chusen Maru*, ex-*Izumi Maru*, which was built as *Kizan Maru* for Kokoku Kisen KK as an original Type 2A. After the three Japanese ownerships she eventually passed to Deh Ling Wu of Hong Kong who registered her to Windhouse S.S. Co. Ltd. of Liberia and renamed her *Fastwind*, no doubt creating a little humour when seen around the waterfronts. As a rebuild she was fitted out to look like one of the earlier style postwar bulk carriers, with machinery remaining aft, but with a very modern accommodation structure and wheelhouse. Cargo handling gear was conventional and in the second photo she is evidently under charter to Kawasaki Line, whose colours she displays on her funnel. (R.J. Tompkins Collection)

Vessel Name	GRT	Completion date	Official number	Builder	Yard #	Machinery	First owner
Yamazono Maru	6,948 grt	28.9.44	ON52679	Harima	348	R	Yamashita Kisen

Completed as a tanker (2AT). 15.2.45, Converted to dry cargo. Classed postwar by ABS. Retained original profile. 1956, Transferred to Nakamura Kisen, renamed *Asahiko Maru*. 7.60, Broken up at Ube, Japan.

Vessel Name	GRT	Completion date	Official number	Builder	Yard #	Machinery	First owner
Yamazumi Maru (Yamasumi)	6,859 grt	27.3.44	ON50848	Kawaminami	A24	R	Yamashita Kisen

Classed postwar by BV. Remained in original profile. 1956, Transferred to Nakamura Kisen, renamed *Asanami Maru*. 12.63, Broken up in Japan.

Vessel Name	GRT	Completion date	Official number	Builder	Yard #	Machinery	First owner
Yoneyama Maru	6,907 grt	3.7.45	ON56332	Hitachi	not available	T	Itaya Shosen

Converted postwar to three-island type. Classed by BV. 17.11.59, In typhoon in South China Sea. Abandoned. 10.12.59, Salvaged by salvage tug *Taikoo* and arrived Hong Kong. Removed to Japan. 4.60, Broken up at Hiroshima.

Vessel Name	GRT	Completion date	Official number	Builder	Yard #	Machinery	First owner
Yuzan Maru No. 2 (Yusan, Yuusan)	6,856 grt.	29.9.44	ON50891	Kawaminami	A31	R	Yamamoto Kisen

15.11.44 Torpedoed and sunk by US submarine *Jack*, 40 miles SW of Cana, French Indochina.

3A CLASS VESSELS

Vessel Name	GRT	Completion date	Official number	Builder	Yard #	Machinery	First owner
Daifu Maru	7,251 grt	28.12.45	ON55773	Harima	327	T	OSK

Built as a dry cargo ship, (see explanatory notes). 1948, Classification not ascertained from Lloyd's Register, but later classed by NK Register (Nippon Kaiji Kyokai). 1948, Transferred to Kambara Kisen KK. 1964, Broken up in Japan. (See note page 154.)

Vessel Name	GRT	Completion date	Official number	Builder	Yard #	Machinery	First owner
Daisetsu Maru No. 1	7,211 grt	7.4.48	ON52840	Ishikawajima	650	T	OSK

According to modified profile plan produced by the builders, this vessel was built with bridge and all accommodation aft (see reproduction). Classed postwar by BV. Although built for OSK it appears that the ship was under charter to Kawasaki up to the transfer to the new owner before and after transfer in 1948. 1948, Transferred to Asahi Kisen KK. 1958, Converted to diesel power. 4.64, Broken up at Onomichi, Japan.

Vessel Name	GRT	Completion date	Official number	Builder	Yard #	Machinery	First owner
Tobata Maru	7,243 grt	15.5.45	ON54578	Harima		T	NYK

Completion 6.22.45. 1948, Transferred to Kyoritsu Kisen KK. Renamed *Kyoshin Maru*. Gross registered tonnage reduced to 6,824. Class not ascertainable from Lloyds Register. Later classed by NK. 1964, Broken up in Japan. (See note page 154.)

Vessel Name	GRT	Completion date	Official number	Builder	Yard #	Machinery	First owner
Tonegawa Maru	7,222 grt	25.5.46	ON55697	Mitsubishi	694	T	Toyo Kaiun

Converted postwar to three-island type. Classed by ABS. 1965, Broken up in Japan.

| *Wayo Maru* | 7,114 grt | 8.8.45 | ON55681 | Mitsubishi | 692 | T | Baba Kisen |

Converted postwar to three-island type. Classed by ABS. 3.61, Broken up in Japan.

| *Yoko Maru* | 7,224 grt | 15.2.46 | ON55688 | Mitsubishi | 693 | T | Taiyo Kaiun |

Transferred to Taiyo Kogyo (a sister company). 1956, Transferred to Mitsui Senpaku. 1958, Transferred to Toyo Kaiun, renamed *Kinugawa Maru*. 1964, Last entry in Lloyds Register. 5.64, Broken up in Japan.

Cancellations

Chiyoda Maru	Ishikawajima	692		T	Nanyo
Shoko Maru	Ishikawajima	693		T	Taiyo

Daisetsu Maru No. 1 was the last and only Type 3A from this builder and it is probable that these two cancelled vessels had the same new profile.

EXPLANATORY NOTES

Classification Issues

Of the forty-eight ships that survived the war or were completed postwar, thirty were taken into dockyard hands and in a remarkable piece of ship surgery were converted to three-island type ships with main machinery removed from aft to amidships. No record is easily ascertainable as to the dates when the rebuilds were completed, beyond noting that this process started as soon as conditions permitted and arrangements could be made with the American administration, classification societies and shipyards. So far as can be ascertained, all were completed by the early 1950s.

Notes to this effect in shipping registers are not always reliable as Lloyd's Register, for example, sometimes did not receive notification until well after the fact, as classification of this group was done by other societies. The delay could be as much as two years. All classification societies went through an unusually busy period after the war, catching up with the confusion of war, particularly in ex-enemy shipping.

Classification was undertaken on all of the postwar survivors under the supervision of the two international societies, American Bureau of Shipping and Bureau Veritas, to bring the ships up to acceptable peacetime commercial standards. Later the Japanese register, Nippon Kaiji Kyokai (NK) took over from the non-Japanese societies. Gross registered tonnages are those indicated when the ships were first built or recorded in Lloyds. Later surveys and changes in the vessels sometimes led to new grts being allocated.

With few exceptions, the newly classed ships appear to have been allotted a maximum twenty-year life from their year of build. The ships were sent to the breakers as their twentieth anniversary, or fifth quadrennial survey, came due. Classification details as they apply to each of the postwar survivors are set out in the individual vessel histories.

Language and Translation Factors

The difficulty in dealing with ship names shows up in a variety of ways. Minor spelling differences between one ship and another have to be watched for and can be confusing, particularly among the many vessels that were operated by NYK and OSK. Examination of the names will make this point clear. The builder's hull number and official number therefore have extra value for resolving any doubt over identity.

Another complication is the differences which arise in the English versions of individual ship names. The identifying initial letter "D" sometimes becomes "T" in the OSK vessels and for this reason any of the OSK vessels might have been recorded with a T. These possible changes in OSK names have not been noted in the fleet list. Most other identified spelling variations have been noted in brackets with the vessel name in the fleet list. These variations are not necessarily right or wrong. They arise because of differing standards of translation and to some extent the application of phonetic spelling. There is no doubt that a good working knowledge of the Japanese language is a valuable tool. It is one the author lacks and in that regard a note from correspondent friend, R.J. Tompkins is particularly helpful. Mr. Tomkins set out the following:

> The Japanese were no different in naming their ships, with individual companies each having its own system of nomenclature such as Port, City, American Presidents and so on.
>
> There was one added and nearly insurmountable problem with the warbuilt ships: they were obviously not in Lloyds and therefore there was no lead to go by until after the war in 1948 and 1949 when they were checked by the surveyors and admitted (to registers). From that time it was possible to identify the particular reading and meaning of the Kanji names used by particular companies.
>
> The first name listed, HAYAHI of Daido Line, means that this company used 'Hi' as the reading or pronunciation of the character in preference to the alternative 'Nichi', 'Jitsu', and 'ka'. All are alternatives for either 'day' or 'sun'.
>
> Simple isn't it?
>
> That therefore makes the Daido ships, AMAHI, HAYAHI, SHIRAHI and TOYOHI (all of which were war losses), because the registration of MUKAHI (the sole survivor) with Lloyds reveals the pattern being used by that particular company.

Mr. Tompkins quotes a friend who was an authority on the Japanese language:

> Transliteration has presented several problems, mainly brought about by the uncertainty of readings [most characters can be read in a number of different ways] of Japanese names.
>
> The simplest example can be given with Nippon and Nihon which are written exactly the same, but are pronounced differently, one soft and the other harsh. In case of uncertainty clarification is usually obtained by consulting other native speakers [though the same problem still applies with native speakers]. Another way to establish the beginning of a word, is to note its position in the index

Mr. Tompkins goes on to add:

> I have used a number of sources to clarify a name including whenever possible a company history as most histories covering the war period printed the ship's name in both Kanji and

Kyoshin Maru. Built as *Tobata Maru*, of the Type 3A, she appears to have most of the attributes of a 2A, including a slightly larger boxlike midships bridge structure. The goalpost masts may have been as designed for the 3A. The side elevation plan of another 3A, *Daisetsu Maru No. 1*, shows the profile of a 3A as designed. Whether this was used for *Tobata Maru*, or whether she was converted to the profile in the above photo as *Kyoshin Maru* of the Kyoritsu Kisen KK has not been possible to establish. Kyoritsu merged with Shinei Senpaku in 1966 and became part of the Mitsui-OSK group. (VMM)

Romaji [normal Roman lettering]. I do not claim to be infallible in my readings and am still open to confirmation on one at least. This is AMATSUSAN or TENSHINSAN which is open to question and neither version has been used before or since so it remains wide open.

A 1TL tanker was built during the war as AMATSU MARU but in that case the name was spelt in Hiragana script and the Kanji characters were not used, so even with the question above, I still lean towards TENSHINSAN which illustrates the dilemma that a ship researcher finds himself in.

Notes on Name Changes

As well as the two cancellations noted at the end of the fleet list, there were undoubtedly other 3A ships planned in a program that anticipated a longer war, but no record can be found.

Names chosen for individual ships might have changed between the time the building contract was first recorded and the date of launch. This was not unknown on the Allied side as a fair number of Canadian "Fort" names meant for British registration and management became "Parks" at the time of leaving the shipyard. This signified that the original allocation had been changed so that the ship, when commissioned, bore a "Park" name and was placed on the Canadian register.

Japanese archival records indicate that the following ships had the same yard and official number, which may indicate that there was a change of plan in the naming process, but for what reason is not now known. Others might have been mistakes of translation, but considering that the official count is 140 it can be appreciated that the use of only one inaccurate name could cause confusion. It should also be remembered that no record existed in English in any shipping register when any of the war losses occurred. The Japanese had no reason to be concerned about the names of their warbuilt ships in English and none of their war losses among the warbuilt ships found their way into Lloyd's Register. Updating the records was a major job following the war with many ships on the Japanese register still in Lloyds when, in reality, they had been lost.

The following has been set out to help avoid the confusion that sometimes arises when examining wartime Japanese shipping records:

First name at time of becoming operational	Unused recorded archival name
Amahi Maru	Tenjitsu Maru
Daibin Maru	Daitoshi Maru
Daisho Maru (Same yard number)	Yasue/Yusue Maru
Hayahi Maru	Sokujitsu/Shokujitsu Maru
Seiko Maru (same official number)	Yasue/Yusue Maru
Shirahi Maru	Hakujitsu Maru
Shozan Maru	Teruyama Maru
Tatsuhiro Maru	Tatsumaya Maru
Tenshinsan Maru	Amatsusan Maru
Toyohi Maru	Toyonichi Maru
Yamanami Maru	Yamato/Yamasho Maru

The term "archival" can mean any one of the many lists whose authorship is unknown or incorrect. The names have been set out above as much as anything to deflect confusion before it arises.

Dimensional Differences

The dimensions of the three yearly classes of Type A ships are

Type	Overall length	Breadth	Depth
1A	445'10"	59'8"	32'2"
2A	448'8"	59'8"	36'4"
3A	449'0"	59'9"	36'1"

The 1A ship, of which only the three noted in the fleet list were built, marked the transition by adaptation of a peacetime design to a wholly wartime emergency design, which came out in the form of the 2A and 3A.

The only distinguishing feature, other than minor hull measurement changes, in Lloyd's Register as between a 2A and 3A is in the profile, where the midships bridge structure of the 2A is moved aft to form a single structure, and tonnage measurement, which is in the range 6,700 to 6,800 for the 2A and 7,100 to 7,200 for the 3A with adjustments in the deadweight tonnage.

A small subclass of Type A appears to have been built as follows: The length shown is registered length as noted in Lloyd's Register. Registered length is length between perpendiculars.

Daisetsu Maru No. 1 (3A)	1948	7211 grt	419.8' x 56.7' x 36.1'
Etorofu Maru (2A)	1948	6711 grt	419.8' x 59.7' x 36.4'
Ishikarigawa Maru (2A)	1947	6705 grt	419.8' x 59.7' x 36.4'

They are assumed to have been originally projected to the same standard design as the other 2A and 3A type ships. These three ships were latecomers out of the shipyards, perhaps completed from partially assembled fabrications or steel already cut which survived bombing. No explanation can be found for the reduction in length of about 6 feet, from the original, but this probably arose because of adjustments found possible in the completion of the ships as peacetime vessels.

New ships built to peacetime designs started to appear around 1949, but prior to that rehabilitation of prewar and warbuilt survivors was doubly important and took top priority as the quickest means of getting ships back into commercial service.

Only one 3A was completed prior to the surrender. This was *Wayo Maru*.

Among the 2A type, *Tatsuyo Maru*, *Toshikawa Maru* and *Yamaji Maru* all show a lesser gross tonnage by about 400 tons. There is no established explanation for this other than the measurable internal spaces used for tonnage calculations must have been different in some detail. All three ships were built by three separate yards and none survived the war, so there are no register entries to work with.

The Najin, Korea losses

The 9th August, 1945 was an expensive day for NYK. Just when the war was very close to its end, *Edamitsu Maru*, *Erimo Maru* and *Enpo Maru* were bombed and sunk by US planes. Interest has been

S.S. DAISETSU-MARU NO.1
CAPACITY PLAN & DEADWEIGHT SCALE

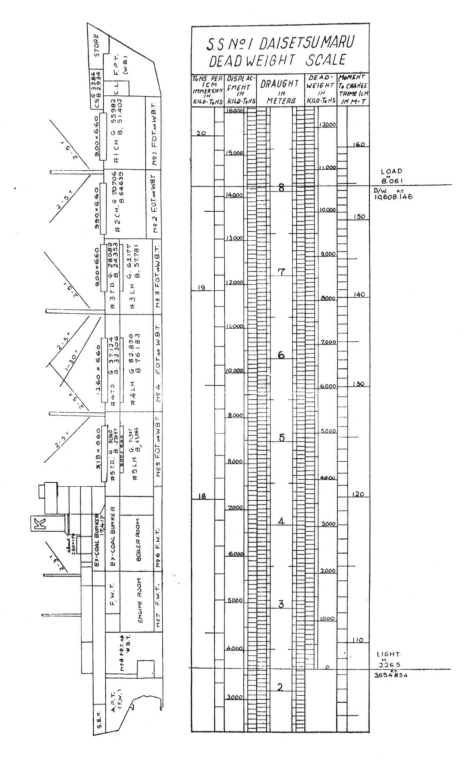

S.S. DAISETSU-MARU NO.1 PARTICULARS

Tonnage :

Gross Ton	7,088.71 T		
Net Ton	3,844.51 T		
D/W	Summer	10,608.15 KT	(10,441 LT)
	Tropical	10,936 KT	(10,763 LT)
	Winter	10,280 KT	(10,118 LT)

Type, Class & Port of Registry etc. :

Type	Well Decker Aft Engine.
Class	B.V. N.K.
Owner	Asahi Kisen Kaisha, Ltd
Port of Registry	Kobe
Call Sign	JAKW
Navigation Area	Ocean Going
Date of Launching	1948
Builder	Ishikawajima Heavy Industries Co.

Principal Dimension :

L.O.A.	137.33 M
L.B.P.	127.96 "
Breadth	18.20 "
Depth	11.10 "
Loaded Draft	8.061 "

Eng., Consumption & Speed etc. :

Main Engine	Steam Turbine 1 Set
Boiler	Water Tube Boiler 3 Sets
Horse Power	3,500 S.H.P.
Speed	Loaded 9.1
"	In Ballast 9.6

Consumption	F.O.(K.T.)	F.W.	Feed W.
at sea	27.2	4.5	9.2
in port	5.3	4.5	10.5

Cargo Equipment :

Hatch No.	Type	No.	Capacity	Booms
No. 1	Steam.	2	5$	2×5$
No. 2	"	2	"	"
No. 3	"	2	"	"
No. 4	"	4	"	4×5$ 1×30$
No. 5	"	2	"	2×5$
Coal Hatch	"	2	"	2×3$

(W inches)

Constant : 300 K.T.

Capacity of Cargo Spaces :

Compartment		Grain (F³)	Bale (F³)
No. 1	C.H.	55,982.90	51,402.96
No. 2	"	70,706.40	64,639.48
No. 3	L.H.	63,177.94	57,781.75
"	T.D.	28,082.22	24,353.49
No. 4	L.H.	82,896.39	76,183.47
"	T.D.	37,124.85	32,306.52
No. 5	L.H.	71,347.82	65,065.79
"	T.D.	31,360.98	27,697.94
F'cle	C.S.	3,286.88	2,934.38
Total		443,966.38	402,365.78
Ex Coal Bunker		34,836.70	

Capacity of Tanks :

Name of Tanks	Tons (S.G. F.O. 0.935)		
	F.O.	F.W.	S.W.
F. P. T.			299.78
No.1 F.O. or W.B.T.(P&S)	323.74		370.00
No. 2 "	544.64		621.94
No. 3 "	199.82		228.18
No. 4 "	275.98		315.14
No. 5 "	197.14		225.12
No. 6 Feed W.T.		232.98	
No. 7 "		73.81	
No.8 F.O. or W.B.T.(P&S)	517.69		576.75
A. P. T.		227.43	
F. W. T.(P&S)		239.36	
Total	2,059.01	773.58	2,636.91

Complement : Officer, 15 Crew, 41 Passenger, 2

Opposite and above: *Daisetsu Maru No. 1*. Builders' drawings and specifications show the last Type 3A to be completed in 1948. She was built to the order of OSK but by the sketch plan seems to have been intended for a Kawasaki charter from the beginning. In 1949 she passed to Asahi Kisen, a company within the NYK group, but what happened to the Kawasaki charter is not clear. It does however, illustrate the complex dealings within Japanese shipping which are often hard to follow. (Ishikawajima-Harima Heavy Industries)

expressed in their fate as it seemed possible that the Soviets raised the vessels. However, an enquiry to the Russian Embassy in Ottawa, asking that it be forwarded to the Russian maritime authorities brought the response "that no information was available." A further enquiry to the Russian archives at the University of Oregon also brought a negative response.

As there were no facilities in the immediate post war period able to repair these ships in Soviet Siberia and as removal to a Japanese or Hong Kong yard was probably not feasible for logistical as well as political reasons, it seems probable that the three wrecks, if raised, went for scrap. An examination of the USSR fleet list in Lloyd's Confidential Index reveals nothing that would indicate that the ships had been incorporated into that country's merchant fleet.

The Longest Lived Ship

Einin Maru enjoyed a longer life than any of her sisters. In 1953 she went to Taiyo Gyogyo KK for use in the whaling industry. Having already outlived her sisters, she went to Daien Reizo in 1969 for use as a fish factory/freezer ship. Her original Bureau Veritas classification expired in 1963, but as she was not engaged in foreign trade, being in internal use in a wholly Japanese industry, she was probably reclassed as a whale processing vessel, later becoming a fisheries factory ship. Evidently, there were improvements or additions in the hull which enlarged her dimensions and with re-engining to diesel propulsion she was likely reclassed for her new specific use. She lasted until 1976.

Tobata Maru and Daifu Maru

It has been suggested that these two ships were built outside of the program that consisted of all the other vessels listed above. This cannot be verified and, given the reality of the Japanese position which had been worsening rapidly since 1943, it seems somewhat improbable, although if they were completed as fast tankers they did amount to a subgroup. According to a Japanese publication *Tobata Maru* was portrayed as a conventional tanker of a more permanent type with deck catwalks and typical tanker layout. Their turbine machinery was rated at a higher 4,000 hp. This was somewhat different to the 2AT tankers listed above which had multiple large tanks installed in their holds. In the 2A ships the tanks were of a temporary nature and could be removed enabling the ship to revert to dry cargo, as a number did even before the war ended. The photograph of *Tobata Maru* as *Kyoshin Maru* indicates a vessel with improved deckhouses and bridge accommodation amidships but generally very similar to the 2A in original form. Otherwise her dimensions matched the other 3A vessels.

To add confusion to the issue, Ishikawajima-Harima (IHI) confirmed that the ships had been built as general cargo ships and nothing in their information relayed to the author indicated that *Tobata Maru* had ever been outfitted as a tanker. On the other hand at least two NYK books, the last one published around 1990 listed the ship as a 3TA and it is assumed that placing the tank designation ahead of the A type signifies that these two ships were more like a true tankship than the 2AT temporary conversions.

Daifu Maru never carried oil as a cargo and that has been confirmed by a reliable Japanese source. In the absence of any further evidence it seems certain that *Tobata Maru* had likewise never functioned as a tanker and that the reference in the NYK books has been misinterpreted.

CHAPTER EIGHT

BEYOND THE TYPE A: OTHER SHIP TYPES IN THE JAPANESE EMERGENCY STANDARD SHIP PROGRAM

WHILE THE TYPE A SHIPS may be described as the core of this account, the Japanese government's overall plan covered a wide range of shipping from small coasters of the Type F to the large and fast tankers with a deadweight of about 16,000 tons.

As previously mentioned, the numeral 1, 2 or 3 before each type of design refers to each of the three programs of 1943, 1944 and 1945. In general, the ships designated with a "1" represented the connecting link with a prewar ship design. These ships included some utilitarian features not normally expected in a peacetime vessel, although in most cases their derivation from a peacetime design can be easily

In an anchorage. A photo that was evidently taken during a
bombing attack. The ship in the foreground bears a resemblance
to a Type 1B freighter, a conventional machinery amidships
vessel with steam up. (US Official)

A four hatch vessel. This appears to be a Type 1C freighter.
When Japan first began to consider the need for wartime
emergency ships in 1937, both this and the preceding vessel's
designs were typical for that period. Time tested designs from as
long ago as the First World War were taken off the shelf and
modernised with cruiser sterns, raked stems and modernistic
touches to the superstructure. (Japan Archive)

The Type D Freighter. As with other classes there were three yearly programs. The two ships illustrated here are from the third program, Type 3D. They had a good designed speed at 14.5 knots. *Malaya Maru No. 2* (above) was launched May 29, 1945 and probably was not completed until after the war. *Chiyaha Maru* (below), did not appear until 1946. As designed they were probably superior to the Type 2A, having among other refinements a full double bottom. (Mitsubishi)

Shipwreck. An interesting Japanese coaster type wrecked somewhere along the Japanese coast, believed to be a 1F coaster or similar, which was designed in peacetime. The ship's mid-section has been destroyed and the engine room eaten out by heavy wave action. Probably the only thing holding the wreck together is the likelihood that the keel and bottom of the vessel, buried in sand, have retained their strength.
(Jim Scammell)

GENERAL ARRANGEMENT OF THE OIL TANKER **Type 1 TL**

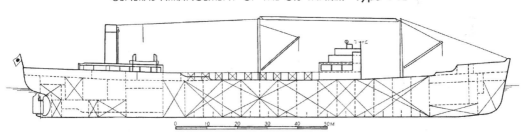

Amatsu Maru. This tanker Type 1TL was a well balanced design that showed off its peacetime origins. (Mitsubishi)

seen. This first annual program had its inception in 1937 when the Japanese government started to give serious consideration to a wartime emergency program. Being conceived in peacetime, it had the imprint of a scheme which had not been exposed to harsh reality. In fact, it is doubtful if any of the peacetime planners had any concept as to just how perilous Japan's merchant shipping position would become in such a short time.

None of the ships in the first program were built in large numbers and in some instances the type was dropped in the second and third programs. Typically, the first program resulted in orders for nine of the Type A ships, but only three 1A were completed. The other six contracts were converted and became the first six 2A in the second program. The 2A was essentially a new design which owed little to its predecessor, except for a close adherence to dimensions, and generally this was the case with the remaining classes which emerged in the second yearly program.

By the time the second program was underway, Japan was feeling severe pressure from a total war at sea, enduring huge losses with appalling frequency. This necessitated much reshaping of the national merchant shipbuilding program. The end result was that the ships in the second and third programs were in every sense utilitarian ships, built with a view to ease of construction and the most economical use of materials. There was literally no room for frills. To facilitate this several of the types in the first annual program were eliminated entirely and Table I in Chapter Five illustrates this point.

The Type TL tankers were produced consistently and being larger and more complex vessels they were not built in great numbers. In spite of the large tanker program there remained a shortage of tankers, which was the reason for adding tank capacity to so many 2A cargo ships, effectively making them temporarily into tankers.

By the second year program of 1944, the 2A, 2D and 2E represented the main output of dry cargo vessels. Their design had been so amended from the predecessor ships in the first year program of 1943 as to be virtually new designs which relied heavily on prefabrication and assembly in large sections.

By the time the second year program began the large tankers were also being fully prefabricated, like the dry cargo ships. The illustrations of the hulls of these vessels clearly show the continuity of design features which appear to have come off the same drawing board.

Conversion of the Type 2A to temporary tankers paralleled similar treatment given to some American Liberties and Canadian Park ships to cover an emergency shortfall. There was no attempt made to create a sophisticated modern tanker with any of them, and as with the Allied ships it was a matter of moving large tonnages of crude or fuel oil. As the Japanese retreat into the home islands took hold in 1945 and particularly after the fall of the Philippines, the need for crude carriers diminished and some of the 2A conversions were quickly reconverted to dry cargo ships, even before the end of the war.

A similar situation arose with the small Type E freighters where, out of a total of 592 units built, 135 were fitted out as tankers.

We have seen how double bottoms were eliminated in the Type A except for the engine rooms. As with the Type 2A, all other types which had previously had engine rooms amidships, moved them as far aft as possible and so far as is known, eliminated or reduced double bottoms in the cargo holds. Moving the machinery aft created a more cramped engine room, but an obvious advantage was elimination of the long propeller shaft. It was easier to create these economies even though more attention had to be

GENERAL ARRANGEMENT OF THE OIL TANKER **Type 1 TM**

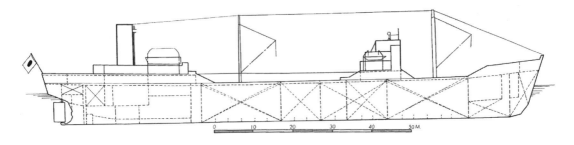

Jambi Maru. The Type 1TM tanker was just a smaller version of Type 1TL. It likewise was a well balanced tanker design. (Mitsubishi)

GENERAL ARRANGEMENT OF THE OIL TANKER **Type 2 TL**

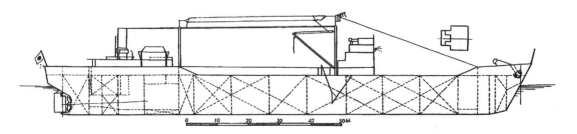

The Type 2TL Tanker. A very similar vessel to the Type 2A freighter, but larger, which also had a tanker version, the Type 2AT. Whereas the 2AT was little more than a freighter with tanks added into the hull which could also be stripped out quickly, the 2TL tanker shown here in side elevation was a tanker, built as such from the keel up. (Mitsubishi)

paid to weight distribution, particularly when the ships were in light condition. This was achieved by installation of larger compensating tanks well forward in the hulls.

The proliferation of smaller ships had much to do with the literally hundreds of small ports and islands with garrisons to be supplied. Also there existed a trade in outbound raw materials, much of which would be transported for transshipment at larger ports such as Singapore, Manila, Rangoon, Saigon, Hong Kong and Batavia (as Djakarta was still known). As wartime conditions worsened, many of the smallest ships had to run the submarine gauntlet in order to supply the home islands of Japan.

Some designs never left the drawing board, notably the 2B, 3E and 3ET. Such details of these as exist are set out in Table 1, Chapter Five. A description of each type actually built, other than the Type A, is given in the following tables.

Note: All measurements are in metres.

Type 1B General Cargo   Coal-fired, turbine engines
  113.09 x 15.8 x 9.1   4,667 grt   7,336 dwt   16 built
  A five-hatch vessel with machinery and accommodation separated from the bridge structure amidships. The profile was split to accommodate coal bunkers and No. 3 hold.
  Welldecks fore and aft. Double bottom throughout. The design was discontinued in the
  second yearly program.

Type 1C General Cargo   Coal-fired, reciprocating engines
  93.83 x 13.70 x 7.6   2,700 grt   4,476 dwt   34 built
  A four-hatch vessel similar to the 1B freighter with accommodation and bridge in one
  island structure amidships. Welldecks fore and aft. Double bottom throughout.
  Discontinued in the third year program.-

Type 1D General Cargo   Coal-fired, reciprocating engines

82.3 x 12.2 x 6.3   1,900 grt   2,850 dwt   22 built

With machinery aft and bridge structure ahead of amidships and a distinct forecastle, the design featured a short No. 1 hatch forward of the bridge and a long No. 2 between the bridge and the machinery aft. The ships of this group had a similar silhouette to larger British coasters. (Not illustrated)

Type 2D General Cargo   Coal-fired, reciprocating engines

85 x 13.40 x 7.2   2,300 grt   4,000 dwt   103 built

In its original form this ship bore no resemblance to the Type D in the second year program. The dimensions were expanded and tonnages substantially increased. Among other changes the bridge structure was moved aft to a single island, all of which was blended into a high poop that was integral with the hull. Unlike the Type 2A, the double bottom was retained over the entire length of the vessel.

Type 3D General Cargo   Coal-fired, turbine engines

98 x 14.30 x 7.5   3,000 grt   4,750 dwt   14 built

In the third year program, the Type D was yet again expanded with a more modest increase in tonnage. By 1945 the ships of this program were looking very like a Type 3A. The biggest difference in profile in the case of the 3D was in the arrangement of its four hatches whereas the 3A had five hatches forward.

Type 1E General Cargo   Diesel engines

| 60 x 9.5 x 5.0 | 830 grt | 1,320 dwt | 14 built |

The E and F types were the only vessels in the wartime programs to be powered by diesels. These classes were coaster-type vessels. The 1E was fitted with a 700 hp hot bulb engine of Japanese design, with machinery amidships and clear welldecks fore and aft, served by derricks mounted at either end of the welldeck. They looked a little like small, Baltic lumber carriers with a counter stern. (Not illustrated)

Type 2E General Cargo   Diesel engines

| 60.44 x 9.5 x 5.45 | 873 grt | 1,581 dwt | 457 built |

When these ships came along they once again presented a radical departure from their predecessor of the previous year's program. The wholly prefabricated hull had the same stark lines of the far larger 2A and 2D with no concave sections in the hull, a heavily angled stemrake and a V type stern. In this design the navigating bridge and all accommodation was concentrated aft above the diesel propulsion machinery. It was the most numerous of all the Japanese designs and, while meant for coastal service, as Japan's position worsened many undertook long voyages between the home country and the furthest limits of conquered lands. They played an important role in the early period after the war in repatriating Japanese servicemen from the many outlying garrisons and getting Japan back to a peacetime economy; but they were not built for a long life.

Type 1F General Cargo   Diesel engines

| 50 x 8.4 x 4.2 | 490 grt | 771 dwt | 21 built |

The smallest of the standard ships, it was discontinued after the first year program. With diesel machinery and accommodation aft its silhouette resembled the 2E but with a counter stern. (Not illustrated)

Type 1K Ore Carrier   Coal-fired, reciprocating engines

| 120 x 16.4 x 10. | 5,244 grt | 6,433 dwt | 20 built |

The deck layout was that of a typical lumber carrier with long, clear welldecks fore and aft and with all cargo handling equipment mounted at the extremities of the wells. However, as a purpose- built ore carrier she would be strengthened in the hull for heavy ore cargoes. The design was dropped after the completion of the first year program. (Not illustrated)

Zuiun Maru. The picture of this 2TL tanker was probably taken in the very worst of circumstances right after peace was declared. Also it was probably taken with a telephoto lens which exaggerated the ugliness of the ship. Despite this she was refurbished after the war and was a unit in the Okada Shosen Kaisha fleet, trading in the Pacific and Far Eastern waters. The goalposts and derricks were probably there for naval auxiliary work. (Mitsubishi)

Yamashio Maru. Her name indicates that this 2TL tanker
converted to an aircraft carrier was meant originally for
Yamashita Kisen. Two of the type were adapted but one was
not completed as an aircraft carrier. The second was found
half sunk when the American occupation forces arrived and
was not deemed worth reconversion to a merchant ship.
She was broken up shortly after the war. (Mitsubishi)

Type 1TS Tanker   Oil-fired, reciprocating engines

65 x 9.96 x 4.72   1,020 grt   1,479 dwt   5 built

A small coastal tanker of conventional appearance, with bridge structure amidships and engines aft. The design was dropped after the first year program as concentration on the 2ET followed in the second year with its large production. (Not illustrated)

Type 1TL Large Tanker   Oil-fired, turbine engines

153 x 20 x 11.5   9,977 grt   15,600 dwt   23 built

A continuation of a peacetime series which had been developed in the 1930s as naval auxiliary tankers and long-distance carriers of crude oil from distant sources. The Japanese tankers of this type built in the 1930s had up to 3,000 tons greater capacity and were about three knots faster than comparable Allied units. They were possibly a factor for consideration when the USMC developed the designs for the highly successful T2 tankers and the British designed one class of its Empire type tankers to a similar specification for use as the Wave class of naval auxiliaries. Two were taken in hand for conversion to escort carriers. (Not illustrated)

Type 2TL Large Tanker   Oil-fired, turbine engines

148 x 20.4 x 12   9,951 grt   16,600 dwt   33 built

The same remarks apply to this group as with the 1TL described above. Two were taken in hand for conversion to escort carriers. (See side elevation plan on page 161.)

Type 3TL Large Tanker   Oil-fired, turbine engines

150.78 x 20.4 x 12   9,961 grt   15,067 dwt   5 built

By the time the third year program for 1945 got underway, Japanese shipbuilding efforts were flagging partly as a result of bombing, but more importantly a mounting shortage of shipbuilding steel and other materials. Of the five in this group, one was taken in hand for completion as an aircraft carrier.

Type 1TM Medium Tanker   Oil-fired, turbine engines

    120 x 16.3 x 11.5 6,400 grt 10,425 dwt 26 built

    The same general remarks apply to this size and class of tanker as with the 1TL and 2TL
groups above. (See side elevation plan on page 163.)

Type 2TM Medium Tanker   Oil-fired, turbine engines

    93 x 13.8 x 7.3 2,850 grt 4,722 dwt 43 built

    Following the pattern with other types, the adoption of the 2TM was a radical jump from
the designated vessel in the first annual program immediately preceding. (Not illustrated)

Type 2ET Small Tanker   Diesel engines

    60.44 x 9.5 x 5.45 873 grt 1,581 dwt 135 built

    As with the dry cargo version, this design became the main focus of the war effort in
terms of small tankers. They were cheaply and quickly built as expendable ships where
quantity took precedence over quality. Probably few of them had a long life.
(Not illustrated)

Tenyo Maru. Built as *Hirito Maru*, this ship was a unit of the 3TL group. The differences between a 2TL and 3TL were not easily apparent, although it is clear that the bow and stem were modified. The occupying power controlled shipping and shipbuilding in the immediate aftermath of the war, but as the Japanese nation was suffering the results of a very poor wartime diet, special allowance was made for building fishing and whaling vessels in order to supply food. This ship was launched for Taiyo Gyogyo, the large whaling concern, as a tanker, but was taken in hand for conversion to a whale meat carrier including the installation of refrigeration equipment. (Mitsubishi)

Top: *Nisshin Maru No. 1*. Originally planned as a 3TL tanker, this ship was completed as a whale oil factory for Taiyo Gyogyo in late 1946. Again it was part of the program for improving the diet of the Japanese people. The visible reminder of her origins as a wartime standard tanker was mainly to be found at the stern where the straight sided shell plating of the original hull can be seen where it meets the whaling ramp. (Mitsubishi)

Bottom: *Yamamizu Maru No. 5*. This 3TL tanker was built for Yamashita Kisen in 1945. The boxlike structure that is the midship accommodation and bridge is very similar to that installed on the Type 2A freighters. This tanker was transferred to Taiheiyo Kaiun KK, a company closely associated with the whaling industry. (Mitsubishi)

Aircraft Carriers from Tankers

Japan's serious deficiency in convoy protection during the early years of the war has been noted in an earlier chapter. As with the highly effective British and American developments in providing convoy protection with escort carriers converted from tankers and freighters, the Japanese diverted a number of their wartime standard tankers for this purpose. Of the five conversions started, none saw active service, having been either damaged or stayed before completion as carriers. Some were ordered by the army because it felt that the navy was unable to provide protection. The entire program was surrounded by much confusion, with conversion followed by reconversion. The ships were too few and too late to have any effect on the progress of the war had they seen completion. These ships are described below.

Shimane Maru	Type 1TLLaunched by Kawaskai (17.12.44) for Ishihara Sangyo KK. Work progressed until plans changed when she was projected to be finished as a cargo ship. Bombed and severely damaged, construction was abandoned and the ship was scrapped postwar.
Otakisan Maru	Type 1TLLaunched by Kawasaki (14.1.45) for Mitsui Bussan. Plans changed for completion as a cargo ship. Adrift and sunk by mine off Kobe (25.8.45).
Yamashio Maru	Type 2TLCompleted by Mitsubishi (Jan 1945) as an escort carrier, but plans cancelled and projected for reconversion to a cargo ship. Bombed, severely damaged and partly sunk. Scrapped postwar.
Chigusa Maru	Type 2TLLaid down in September, 1944. Work stopped and the hull remained on the ways until two years later. Completed as a cargo ship.
No name known	Type 3TLTaken over while under construction. Turbine ship with projected speed of 19 knots. Conversion never completed.

Output of the Japanese Steel Shipbuilding Industry

The Emergency Standard Ship program, in addition to other wartime requirements, entailed the full shipbuilding resources of the country. The bigger yards were obviously the most suited to the bigger ships, but the smaller classes were spread throughout the nation's fifty-seven steel shipbuilding yards. Output, as nearly as it can be established, is set out below. This is based on an inventory organized by the SCAJAP shortly after the war and labelled *Japanese Merchant Shipbuilding*. The study was meant to be an assessment of the effectiveness of the strategic bombing undertaken by the US forces. It was published in January 1947, compiled from information supplied on demand from the Japanese shipbuilding industry.

The list had some deficiencies, particularly in the number of vessels actually built. For example, it lists only 130 Type A completed as against 140 actually built, so the figures in the survey may be a little understated. As was noted in the Type A program several of the vessels described in Chapter Seven were completed as late as 1948 and the same position probably arose in some degree with some of the other classes. Disparities are therefore understandable given the state of confusion existing in the immediate aftermath of war.

The yards were graded into six classes measured by the monetary value of their output.

Major Yards	Value Added in Millions of Yen	Number of Yards
Class 1	More than 300	1
Class 2	125-300	5
Class 3	50-125	6-Minor Yards
Class 4	25-50	10
Class 5	10-25	15
Class 6	Less than 10	20

The yards in each class are given below.

	Value all work in Millions of Yen	Merchant ships, total gross tons	Warship, total tonnage displacement
Class 1			
Nagasaki-Mitsubishi	395.4	353,166	149,110
Class 2			
Yokohama-Mitsubishi	267.4	135,315	37,553
Tokyo-Mitsubishi	231.8	183,915	32,240
Tamano-Mitsui	195.0	304,983	17,450
Kobe-Kawasaki	174.7	107,803	52,338
Aioi-Harima	133.4	248,296	45,600
Class 3			
Koyagijima-Kawaminami	104.1	366,977	-
Ishikarigawa	101.1	131,706	7,620
Uraga	100.0	98,689	23,400
Tsurumi-Nippon Kokan	91.0	127,855	35,450
Innoshima-Hitachi	85.4	96,461	1,760
Sakurajima-Hitachi	70.7	97,722	1,905 ·
Class 4			
Hakodate-Hakodate	38.8	39,783	2,456

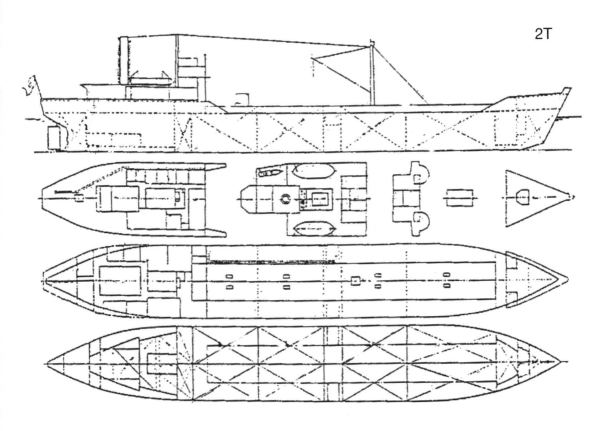

2T

The three side elevation and general arrangement plans of Japanese standard ships shown here are typical of large and small vessels from the second and third programs. No maritime nation involved in WWII embraced the concept of the standard ship so completely as Japan. All seem to have been from the same drawing board with similar hull lines and common features throughout, only adjusted to suit the size and projected employment of each ship.

Spartan features and such economies as the lack of double bottoms, ensured that all the ships had short post-war lives. Exceptions were those, like the Type A and some of the tankers, where rebuilding was justified to give a normal ship life of twenty years.

2D

2E

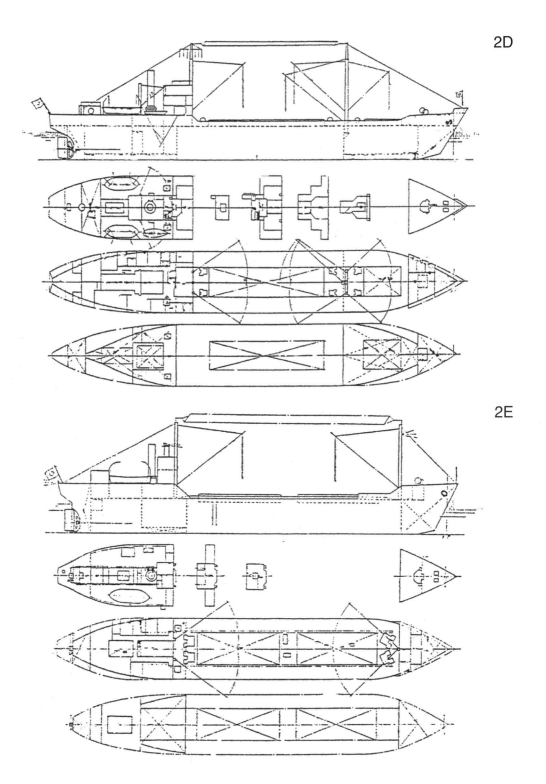

	Value all work in Millions of Yen	Merchant ships, total gross tons	Warship, total tonnage displacement
Fukahori-Kawaminami	38.0	134,950	-
Wakamatsu-Mitsubishi	36.3	117,204	-
Mukashima-Hitachi	35.4	9,340	9,790
Matsunoura-Harima	34.3	138,523	-
Fujinagata	34.3	3,538	32,780
Shimonoseki-Mitsubishi	33.3	12,950	2,294
Naniwa	31.4	27,810	4,010
Hiroshima-Mitsubishi	29.7	48,234	-
Uranosaki-Kawaminami	29.4	25,937	20,450
Class 5			
Nagoya	24.2	49,988	-
Osaka	22.9	23,448	28,726
Chikko-Hitachi (repair)	22.6	-	-
Namura	21.9	28,370	-
Kyushu	21.7	30,858	-
Amagasaki-Amagasaki	20.9	18,840	-
Dairen	20.0	29,079	-
Konan-Mitsubishi	18.9	48,928	-
Senshu-Kawasaki	16.3	-	7,630
Nipponkai	15.4	9,646	3,750
Niigata	14.6	-	6,830
Taguma-Urabe	11.4	25,105	-
Class 6			
Osaka-Amagasaki	8.1	7,281	-
Muroran-Hakodate	6.9	1,204	-
Hayashikane	6.8	6,326	-
Horai	5.9	7,811	300
Tohoku	5.7	6,232	-
Hashihama	5.3	10,700	-
Kisugawa (repair)	5.2	-	-
Kobe-Sanko	4.4	10,844	-
Settsu	4.2	5,460	-
Kanasashi	4.1	3,655	-
Osaka-Sanko	3.8	9,163	-
Ohara	3.7	4,150	286

	Value all work in Millions of Yen	Merchant ships, total gross tons	Warship, total tonnage displacement
Sanoyasu	3.5	23,822	-
Kanagawa-Hitachi	2.9	8,684	-
Shimuzu-Nippon Kokan	2.1	2,300	-
Miho	2.0	2,617	-
Osaka-Urabe	2.0	4,506	-
Tokai	1.4	1,562	-
Kanagawa	.2	300	-
Yokohama	.1	150	--

The dominance of the *Zaibatsu*-controlled yards, such as Mitsubishi, Mitsui, Hitachi and Harima can be readily appreciated by an examination of the second names in the above list. Even most of those without a named affiliation can be assumed in almost all instances to be associated with one or another of the main groups. The sheer size of the Mitsubishi group in shipbuilding can also be appreciated when noting that no less than seven yards carry their name, the largest being the first three in the above list. -After the war new yards came into being, some of which absorbed some of the above names. The big navy yards are not listed as they did not move into merchant shipbuilding until after the war and then were awarded to the big groups. Two of the major yards, Ishikawajima and Harima amalgamated and took over the huge Kure Naval Shipyard to make IHI one of the very largest of the Japanese shipbuilders.

BIBLIOGRAPHY

Alden, John D. *US Submarine Attacks during World War II*. Annapolis, MD: Naval Institute Press, 1989. Includes British and Dutch submarine attacks in the southeast Asian theatre.

Brown, Atholl Sutherland. *Silently Into the Midst of Things*. Lewes, Sussex: The Book Guild Ltd, 1997. An eyewitness account of the RAF rollback of the Japanese in Burma.

Chida, Tomohei and Peter N. Davies. *The Japanese Shipping & Shipbuilding Industries: A History of their Modern Growth*. London: The Athlone Press, 1990.

Clark, Robin et al. *The Australian National Line 1956-81: History and Fleet List*. Kendal, England: The World Ship Society, 1982. Refers to Australian warbuilt standard ships.

Dollinger, Hans. *The Decline and Fall of Nazi Germany and Imperial Japan: A Pictorial History of the Final Days of World War II*. New York: Bonanza Books, MCMLXVII.

Dower, John W. *Embracing Defeat: Japan in the wake of WWII*. New York: W.W. Norton Co., 1999.

Dull, Paul S. *A Battle History of the Imperial Japanese Navy 1941-1945*. Annapolis, MD: Naval Institute Press, 1978.

Enright, Joseph F and James W. Ryan, *Shinano! The Sinking of Japan's Secret Supership*. New York: St. Martin's Press, 1985.

Evans, David C. and Mark R. Peattie. *Kaigun: Strategy, Tactics and Technology in the Imperial Japanese Navy, 1887-1941*. Annapolis, MD: Naval Institute Press, 1997.

Falle, Sam. *My Lucky Life: In War, Revolution, Peace & Diplomacy*. Lewes, Sussex: The Book Guild, 1996.

Harvey, Robert. *The Undefeated; The Rise, Fall and Rise of Greater Japan*. London: Macmillan Limited, 1994.

Heal, S.C. *A Great Fleet of Ships: The Canadian Forts and Parks*. St. Catharines, ON: Vanwell Publishing Ltd, 1999. Explains the concept of the standard ship.

Howarth, Stephen. *The Fighting Ships of the Rising Sun: The Drama of the Imperial Japanese Navy, 1895-1945*. New York: Atheneum, 1983.

Kinsman, William. *Before I Forget*. Published privately, Victoria, BC 1993. A personal memoir on the author's career in the Royal Navy with particular reference to the British submarine activity in South East Asia.

McCracken, David R. *Four Months of a Jap Whaler*. New York: Robert M. McLeod & Co, 1948. A useful insight into living with a Japanese crew in the aftermath of the Second World War.

Mitchell, W.H. and L.A. Sawyer. *British Standard Ships of World War I*. Liverpool: The Journal of Commerce & Shipping Telegraph Ltd, 1968. Explains the British N class standard ship program in the First World War which the author theorises may have been the Japanese source of inspiration in developing the Type A standard ship program of the Second World War.

Noma, Hisashi. *Japanese Merchant Ships at War: The Story of Mitsui and OSK Liners Lost During the Pacific War*. Published privately by the author in Japan in 2002.

Parillo, Mark P. *The Japanese Merchant Marine in World War II*. Annapolis: Naval Institute Press, 1993.

Patric, John. *Why Japan Was Strong*. New York: Doubleday, Doran & Co., 1943.

Roberts, John G. *Mitsui: Three Centuries of Japanese Business*. New York & Tokyo: Weatherill, 1973.

Scalia, Mark. *Germany's Last Mission to Japan: The Failed Voyage of U 234*. Annapolis: Naval Institute Press, 2000.

Center of Military History, US Army. *The United States Army in World War II: The War Against Japan*. Washington, DC: Brassey's Five Star Paperbacks, 1994.

Military Supply Division, US Army. *The United States Strategic Bombing Survey: Japanese Merchant Shipbuilding*. New York: Republished by UMI Books on Demand, 1947.

Voyage of a Century. Photograph Collection of NYK ships. Tokyo: Nippon Yusen Kaisha, 1985. Lists NYK losses during the Pacific War.

SHIP INDEX

*photographs in bold

GENERAL INDEX